S0-BSI-112

Christmas 2004

To a fellow Cardinals fan
and a great Dad — it's been
fun to share sports and life
with you!

Love,
Morgan

Whitey's Boys

A Celebration of the
'82 Cards World Championship

Rob Rains
Alvin A. Reid

TRIUMPH
BOOKS
CHICAGO

Copyright © 2002 by Rob Rains and Alvin A. Reid

No part of this publication may be reproduced, stored in a retrieval system, or trans-mitted, in any form by any means, electronic, mechanical, photocopying, or other-wise, without the prior written permission of the publisher, Triumph Books, 601 S. LaSalle St., Suite 500, Chicago, Illinois, 60605.

Just as this book was going to press, all Cardinals fans were shocked and saddened by the death of Darrell Porter, the catcher for the 1982 world champion Cardinals and the MVP of the World Series. He was interviewed for the book in May 2002. The authors would like to dedicate this book to his memory.

Library of Congress Cataloging-in-Publication Data

Rains, Rob.
    Whitey's boys : a celebration of the '82 Cards world championship / Rob Rains, Alvin A. Reid.
       p. cm.
    Includes index.
    ISBN 1-57243-485-6 (hc)
      1. St. Louis Cardinals (Baseball team)—History. 2. World Series (Baseball) (1982) I. Reid, Alvin A., 1960– II. Title.

GV875.S3 R355 2002
796.357'64'0977866—dc21

2002072537

This book is available in quantity at special discounts for your group or organization. For further information, contact:
Triumph Books
601 South LaSalle Street
Suite 500
Chicago, Illinois 60605
(312) 939-3330
Fax (312) 663-3557

Printed in the United States of America
ISBN 1-57243-485-6
Interior design by Sue Knopf

Contents

Foreword   by Whitey Herzog v

Chapter 1   Joaquin Andujar 1

Chapter 2   Bob Forsch. 9

Chapter 3   David Green 17

Chapter 4   George Hendrick 21

Chapter 5   Keith Hernandez 31

Chapter 6   Tom Herr 39

Chapter 7   Dane Iorg 49

Chapter 8   Tito Landrum 53

Chapter 9   Dave LaPoint. 63

Chapter 10 Willie McGee. 73

Chapter 11 Ken Oberkfell 81

Chapter 12 Darrell Porter 87

Chapter 13 Mike Ramsey. 93

Chapter 14 Lonnie Smith. 99

Chapter 15 Ozzie Smith. 107

Chapter 16 John Stuper 117

Chapter 17 Bruce Sutter. 127

Appendix I   Newspaper Coverage of the Cardinals' Championship . . . 133

Appendix II Statistical Tables: Pitchers 161

Appendix III Statistical Tables: Hitters 177

Index 211

Foreword

Editor's note: Whitey Herzog became the St. Louis Cardinals' manager midway through the 1980 season after several winning years managing the Kansas City Royals. St. Louis had the worst record in the major leagues when he was hired in June of 1980. Later in the season, Herzog took on the additional role of general manager. In the strike-shortened season of 1981, Herzog's first full year as manager, the Cardinals finished with the best total winning percentage in the National League's Eastern Division but missed the playoffs as they finished each half of the season in second place.

In an effort to focus solely on his managerial duties, Herzog stepped down as general manager on Opening Day of 1982. The move paid off as the Cardinals claimed their first National League East Championship. A 3–0 National League Championship Series sweep of the Atlanta Braves put the Cardinals in their 13th World Series against the Milwaukee Brewers, who fell 4–3 to St. Louis in the fall classic. As a big-league manager, Herzog won six division titles, three pennants, and the 1982 World Series. The accomplishments of the 1982 team were especially satisfying to him. Although they hit only 67 home runs, the fewest in the major leagues, the 1982 Cardinals never lost more

*than three games in a row until after winning the division
championship.*

Twenty years should seem like a long time. Even though that is
how long it has been since the 1982 Cardinals won the World
Series, in many ways it does not seem that long ago.

I have been privileged to manage a lot of great teams during my
lifetime, but there are several reasons why the 1982 club is so special to me. First of all, it was my first team that ever reached the World
Series, and then we won the championship. There is no feeling in
the world quite like knowing that you are the world champions. One
of my most prized possessions is a photograph of me and Gussie
Busch, taken in my office the night we won the Series. We are both
grinning from ear to ear.

I have had the honor of managing some wonderful players over
the years. Two of them are now in the Hall of Fame: George Brett
and Ozzie Smith. When I was able to talk Jack McKeon into trading
Ozzie to the Cardinals for Garry Templeton, I had no idea I was obtain-
ing a future Hall of Famer. It is true I told Ozzie that if he agreed to
come to St. Louis I thought we could win a World Series, and that's
exactly what happened.

Getting Ozzie completed the changes that had to be made to make
the Cardinals a winning team. When I became the manager in 1980,
the organization was floundering badly and there was much turmoil
in the front office. Everybody thought they were going to be fired.
People were misplaced. The ballclub was last in the division, even
though it had a lot of potential.

It took only a few games for me to realize it was a one-base team.
I was sitting in my office after a game, about a week after I had taken
over, when Butch Yatkeman, our clubhouse and equipment guy,
brought me a Budweiser. I said, "Dang it, Butch, it takes us four hits
to get a run." He said, "Whitey, this is the slowest team and the worst
base-running team I've ever seen, and I've been here 57 years."

Butch was right. At that time in baseball, nobody was hitting a lot
of home runs, and they certainly weren't being hit at Busch Stadium.

We didn't have the kind of players who could take advantage of our ballpark. We needed guys who could run, who could play defense, and we needed pitchers who could utilize those strengths—don't walk people, and get the batter to hit the ball on the ground.

That was the way we tried to remake the ballclub. Did I know we were going to be so successful so quickly? No. But I knew we had acquired the right types of players—the players who would give us a chance to win—and that was the promise I had made to Gussie when he gave me the job.

The first move I made was to sign Darrell Porter as our catcher. Darrell had played for me in Kansas City, and I knew he would be a great addition to our lineup. He was one of those special kinds of players who just had a knack for playing baseball. He was a winner. People in St. Louis didn't like the move at first, because they were in love with Ted Simmons. Ted was a wonderful guy and has had a nice career both as a player and now in the front office, but he just didn't fit the needs of our ballclub. If we had been an American League club, Ted would have been a lifelong Cardinal because he would have been perfect as a DH.

My original idea after getting Darrell was to move Ted to first base and switch Keith Hernandez to left field. Ted was originally OK with the move, but then he had second thoughts about it. I think he was afraid that Keith was so good at first—one of the best I had ever seen— that if he made a mistake people would compare him to Keith. He thought Keith might even be laughing at him out in left field, so he came back a few days later and said he wanted to be traded.

That left Keith at first, which was fine with me. As I said, he might have been one of the best fielding first basemen ever, and I thought if we could surround him with better players, especially guys who could get on base in front of him, he would really be able to drive in some runs for us.

Ken Oberkfell was our second baseman, and Obie was outstanding. The only problem we had was that Tommy Herr was coming up through the system and was about ready for the majors, and he needed to play second. When we were able to trade Ken Reitz and

Leon Durham to the Cubs for Bruce Sutter, that allowed me to move Obie to third and put Tommy at second.

Garry Templeton was playing shortstop when I came to St. Louis. He might have been one of the most talented players I ever managed, but once he got in trouble, making some obscene gestures to the crowd during a game in 1981, I knew we had to make a move. San Diego was willing to make the deal, and I am happy Garry was able to play there and do a good job for a long time. He has been managing in the minor leagues for several years now, and I am happy for him.

Getting Ozzie to play short gave us arguably the best infield in the game. Nobody really talks about it much, but that was so important to us winning. We didn't lose games very often. If the other team won, they had earned it by beating us. My old boss Casey Stengel used to say teams lost more games than they won, but that definitely wasn't true with this team.

The guy we got to be our offensive catalyst was Lonnie Smith, who had been with the Phillies. He played left, and he was an exciting player. You never knew what he was going to do, but more times than not, he ended up making the play or stealing the base or driving in the run that won the game. In center field we had one of the best prospects in the history of the game, David Green, who had come over from the Brewers in the Simmons trade.

David might have been a couple of years older than we thought he was, because I don't know anybody who has ever seen his birth certificate from Nicaragua. He could do everything, but unfortunately he ran into some personal problems that kept him from becoming the player I thought he would turn out to be.

One of the biggest breaks we got in 1982 came when David got hurt in May. We thought he was going to be out a couple of weeks so we put him on the disabled list and called up a kid we had obtained from the Yankees, Willie McGee. I remember telling Willie not to get too comfortable, because he was probably going to be here for only a couple of weeks and then would be going back to Louisville. He stayed in St. Louis for most of the next 18 years he played in the big leagues.

"Silent" George Hendrick was our right fielder. He was known mostly for his refusal to talk to the press, but that didn't bother me. He was a very solid, dependable guy and was really our only legitimate power hitter, even though power then meant 20 homers instead of 50.

Going into the 1982 season, I was very content with our starting lineup. We also had added some good guys for our bench, which is often an underrated reason for a team's success. We had Gene Tenace, who had been on winning clubs in Oakland, as our backup catcher, and Mike Ramsey was our key utility infielder. He was a very solid guy whom I knew I could count on when I needed to give one of our regulars a rest. We had Steve Braun and Dane Iorg as our veteran pinch-hitters, and both of them knew exactly what their role was and were prepared even before I told them to get ready to hit. Tito Landrum was a young player then who was happy to be there and ready to do whatever we asked of him.

I did have some concerns about our pitching staff. I knew Bob Forsch and Joaquin Andujar, whom we had acquired from Houston right before the strike in 1981, would be two of the starters. I thought another would be Andy Rincon, a promising young pitcher, but he had gotten hurt the year before and was never the same after that.

We started the season with Eric Rasmussen and John Martin in the rotation, along with Steve Mura, who had come over from San Diego. By the middle of May, we made a couple of changes and put two rookies in the rotation—Dave LaPoint and John Stuper. They both did a great job for us.

The beauty of that pitching staff was that I really had to worry only about seven innings, because we had Sutter in the bullpen. I knew he could go the last two innings. My goal every game was to get a 3–2 lead after the seventh inning, and I knew we were going to win nine out of ten times.

We had Doug Bair and Jim Kaat as our setup guys, and they came up with some big performances for us too. Everybody, it seemed, stepped up and did a job when we asked them to. I don't think I was surprised by anybody's performance. They all did what we thought they could do.

I was fortunate to have a good staff of coaches on that club. Chuck Hiller was our third-base coach and Hal Lanier coached first. Hub Kittle was the pitching coach, and the pitchers loved him, especially Joaquin. Red Schoendienst was on the bench with me, and Dave Ricketts was in the bullpen. I don't know how many hours of batting practice Dave threw that season, but he was always available every time somebody needed some extra work.

I really think one of the best things about that team was they were all good guys. I think it might have been the only team I ever managed that I didn't have to chew out the group as a whole the whole season. We had some individual problems that came up, as they always do, but those were small and were taken care of privately.

We could do so many things to manufacture runs. Some of the media came up with a new term for the way we played—"Whiteyball." Whatever they wanted to call it was fine, as long as we were winning.

Our guys really knew how to play. We always did so many things defensively to take runs away from the other team. We never failed to execute. When there was a man on second base with no outs, we got him to third. I think we squeezed 17 times that year and scored 14 runs. We had two foul balls and one out.

Those guys weren't worried about money, what they were going to be making next year. They just wanted to play and have a good time, and that's what they did.

We started the season by beating Nolan Ryan in Houston, and good things continued to happen from there. A 12-game winning streak in April convinced everyone we were good enough to win and put the team in a very positive state of mind. We didn't lose more than three games in a row until after we clinched the division title the last week of the season.

We played the same way the entire season—running at every opportunity, playing great defense, and getting good solid pitching from our starters and the bullpen. Only George Hendrick hit more than 12 home runs, finishing with 19, and we hit only 67 as a team, the lowest total in the majors. We stole 200 bases, however, the most in the league, and our pitchers allowed the fewest runs in the league. Our infield combined for just 44 errors for the season. Forsch and Andujar each won 15 games, and Sutter earned 36 saves, remaining the most dominant closer in the game. That was our formula for winning games.

We did win some exciting games on the way to the pennant. Probably the most dramatic was on a Sunday afternoon in August, when we were playing the San Francisco Giants at home. We were tied in the bottom of the twelfth, and Glenn Brummer, our third-string catcher, was on third. David Green was batting, with two outs and a 3–2 count. Brummer took off, trying to steal home. The pitch was right down the pipe, and Dave Pallone was the umpire. He never called it a ball or a strike. To this day he has never called it a ball or a strike. If it was a strike, it was strike three and the inning was over. He called Brummer safe, we won the game, and we got off the field as quickly as possible. The only problem after that was I couldn't put him in to run anymore because he was always trying to steal bases.

In September, we were in the heat of the pennant race with the Phillies when we went to Philadelphia. John Stuper pitched and carried a 2–0 lead into the eighth inning when they loaded the bases. Mike Schmidt was coming up. I went out to the mound to get John and bring in Sutter. I had barely got back to the dugout before Bruce had gotten out of the inning, getting Schmidt to hit into a pitcher-to-home-to-first double play.

We followed that win by going to New York, where, thanks to some earlier rainouts, we had to play back-to-back doubleheaders, a total of five games in three days. Ozzie was hurt, so Ramsey had to play short. He played every inning of every game, he never made an error, and we won all five games. I knew then that we had something special going.

We clinched the division title in Montreal, then faced the Braves in the playoffs. We got a break from the weatherman when the opening game was called because of rain, two outs shy of Atlanta and

Phil Niekro winning 1–0. They couldn't use Niekro again the next day, and we won to start a three-game sweep.

The World Series followed, and it was a great Series. It didn't start out so great with us losing the opener, 10–0, but we battled back. We were losing 3–2 after five games, but Stuper gave us a great effort in Game 6, another game delayed by rain, and we won 13–1 to force the seventh game.

Thanks to some big hits by Hernandez, Hendrick, and Porter, we took a 6–3 lead into the ninth with Sutter on the mound. I felt confident but still was able to exhale only after Bruce struck out Gorman Thomas and Darrell flung his mask in the air as he charged to the mound.

Our theme song for the year had been "Celebration," by Kool and the Gang, and as the song played over the loudspeakers at Busch and our fans were going crazy, it was a special time for all of us. Everybody associated with the 1982 Cardinals will never forget that feeling.

The best thing about that team might have been that they all liked to fish. I spent many a morning on Herb Fox's lake in Illinois with one or more of my players, talking to them, getting to know them, getting to know their families. They were all good players, but more important, they were all good people. I wouldn't trade those memories for anything.

It has been 20 years, even though it seems much less than that. Those guys have all grown older, they have all moved on to other jobs and activities, and we don't get to see each other nearly as often. Some of the guys who stayed in town, like Ozzie, I see fairly often, but there are some players on that team I haven't seen for quite a while. All have interesting stories to tell about what they are doing now and how they have changed over the past 20 years.

As for me, I've been retired for nine years. I still fish for bass and crappie about five days a week. I still see and fish with Herb Fox, but I am sorry to say his beloved wife, Helen, passed away a couple of years ago. She was an angel. I wonder how often during my 10 years with the Cardinals she and Herbie had me and Mary Lou, my coaches, and the players over to their home in Freeburg for some really tremendous fish fries.

Mary Lou and I have been blessed with three great children and now have nine grandchildren—one girl and eight boys. Our granddaughter, Kirsten, will be graduating from college soon. She's 22 years old. Our youngest grandson is 2 years old. His name is Trevor. In between, our grandsons' ages are 20, 18, 13, 12, 8, 5, and 4. We have some athletes, but they are all great kids. Needless to say, we love them dearly.

All of the 1982 team is scheduled to come to town in September 2002 for a charity golf tournament, honoring the 20th anniversary of the 1982 champions. I can't wait to see them. They were a good bunch of guys.

—Whitey Herzog
St. Louis, Missouri

1 | Joaquin Andujar

To those Cardinals fans who remember Joaquin Andujar—and he definitely is a hard guy to forget—what he is doing these days might sound more than a little scary. He is teaching young Dominican players about baseball.

The man whose two most common English phrases in the eighties were "one tough Dominican" and "you never know" operates his school in San Pedro de Macoris in the late afternoons from Monday through Friday. He currently has about 40 players under his tutelage.

"They are young," Andujar said. "I like to work with young people."

Even scarier, Andujar is teaching these potential major league prospects about more than pitching, an area he does know something about.

"I instruct them on everything in baseball," Andujar said. "I try to teach them how to play the game of baseball. How to play the game of baseball right."

Andujar has been back in his native Dominican Republic since retiring as a player after the 1988 season. He is beloved in his home country, as he never forgot where he came from and used his success in the United States to provide clothes, shoes, and baseball equipment to underprivileged youngsters throughout his career. It was not unusual for Andujar to walk around the Cardinals' clubhouse with an empty box, asking teammates if they had any old equipment they would like to donate. As soon as the box was full, he would ship it off to the Dominican Republic.

Just as there was no denying his love for the Dominican Republic, there also is no denying Andujar's love of baseball. He said that ever since retiring, even though he has remained active in the game, he has missed it.

"If you play for money, you don't care," Andujar said. "But if you play for love, and I love the game of baseball, then you miss it a lot."

Andujar said he "did nothing" after he retired except stay home and be with his family.

"I would go to the ballpark every day, though," he said.

His son, Jesse, also spent many days at the ballpark. He is now a pitcher with the California League Class A Rancho Cucamonga Quakes. The younger Andujar pitched against one of his father's 1982 teammates, George Hendrick, the manager of the Lake Elsinore Storm, during the season.

"I just let him alone. I let him play," Andujar said. "When he makes the major leagues, then I go see him."

Andujar gave his son his 1982 World Series ring, and Jesse keeps it with him as he makes the minor league bus trips and works his way to a possible major league career.

Joaquin also has another son, Christopher.

Andujar still loves his native Dominican Republic, saying, "I always live here; I never leave here during my career. I want to be here for young people. The game of baseball is special here. I want to keep it that way. I want to teach baseball."

What Andujar is doing now doesn't surprise Whitey Herzog. In fact, when Herzog was running the California Angels in the early 1990s, he hired Andujar as a scout in the Dominican Republic.

"He did a good job," Herzog said. "Joaquin could be a great scout. He really knows talent."

Herzog said he will never forget the first time he walked into the ballpark in the Dominican Republic, where Andujar had arranged for several young prospects to come work out and play a game while Herzog was there.

"Joaquin was throwing batting practice, and he was really cutting it loose," Herzog said. "All of those 16-year-old kids couldn't touch him. They had never seen a guy throwing 80–85 miles an hour before. He thought he was throwing 95.

"I said, 'Joaquin, what are you doing?' He said, 'Whitey, I can still pitch in the big leagues. I can still throw 95.' I told him he couldn't throw 95 in his prime. He said for me to get out the radar gun and he would show me after the game."

After the game, Herzog got out the radar gun, and Andujar went and warmed up—and threw 82 miles an hour. "He said, 'That gun ain't worth a damn,'" Herzog said.

It was Herzog's intention with the Angels to scout the Dominican Republic hard, hoping to sign away some of the young players who seemed to always be going to other organizations. The Dominican Republic has always been a hotbed for talent, and Herzog thought the Angels were at a disadvantage because they did not have more of a presence in the country.

San Pedro de Macoris is a seaport with much heavy industry, but it is best known in the United States as the birthplace of many major league stars. In addition to Andujar, the city has produced scores of great players, including Juan Marichal, Pedro Martinez, Sammy Sosa, Julian Javier, Felipe Alou and his sons, Rico Carty, Mario Soto, Manny Mota, Tony Fernandez, Tony Peña, Manny Ramirez, and Jose Rijo.

"San Pedro de Macoris became a religion, something for every area of our country to emulate," Ellis Perez, a former minister of tourism, a government adviser, and an entrepreneur, said in a Dominican Republic tourism press kit.

"The Dodgers, Giants, Expos, Pirates, and other big-league teams now maintain year-round training camps in the Dominican Republic, developing the baseball stars of tomorrow."

Early in the 2002 season, there were 314 natives of the Dominican Republic playing in the major leagues, the most of any country other than the United States.

Herzog arranged for the Angels to build a stadium in the Dominican Republic. It was going to be complete with a dormitory, classrooms, and a kitchen, and the idea was that the Angels would bring in these young players, house them, and teach them, then sign them when they became old enough.

"I told Joaquin 'get out of the capital,'" Herzog said. "'Go up in the jungle and find out who can run and throw. We'll teach them for two years and then sign them.'"

One of Andujar's jobs was to oversee the construction of the stadium; he also runs a construction company in his native country. Herzog was in for a big surprise one day when he received a phone call with the news that Andujar had fired the entire construction crew that morning.

When Herzog reached Andujar on the telephone, he said, "'Joaquin, who is going to finish the stadium?' He said, 'I am.'"

The stadium did finally get built, but Herzog's plan of investing heavily in the Dominican Republic never materialized because the Angels' owners were against it. Andujar eventually was fired as a scout, not because of a lack of effort, but because he was doing too much.

"I tried to reach him one day and found out he was in New York," Herzog said. "He said, 'I got a tip about a prospect.' I told him we had scouts in New York too, who probably had heard about the kid."

The relationship between Herzog and Andujar was born when the Cardinals acquired Andujar from the Astros for outfielder Tony Scott just before the strike in 1981. Herzog made the deal with the encouragement of pitching coach Hub Kittle, who had worked with Andujar in Houston.

Andujar soon began referring to Herzog as "my daddy," and he continues to call him that to this day.

"We became pretty tight," Herzog said. "He had three really good years for us."

The first of those years was in 1982, when Andujar tied Bob Forsch for the staff lead with 15 victories and turned in a 2.47 ERA, striking out 137 batters while walking only 50. He also allowed only 11 home runs.

Forsch found Andujar to be everything he had expected.

"My brother Ken played for Houston, and I asked him what was up with this guy," Forsch said. "He told me he was a live wire. He was always in the mix. He kept things going in the clubhouse, but in a fun way."

It was always easier to have fun when you were winning, which is why Andujar became the victim of numerous clubhouse pranks and practical jokes. When he was serious, however, there was no tougher competitor on the mound than Andujar.

Andujar was working on a shutout in the seventh inning of Game 3 of the World Series, when he was hit on the right kneecap by a line drive off the bat of Ted Simmons and had to be carried off the field.

When the Series was extended to seven games, Andujar was scheduled to be the starting pitcher for the Cardinals. Herzog was unsure if he would be able to pitch, however, so he also had rookie Dave LaPoint warming up alongside Andujar just in case LaPoint had to start.

"The biggest problem was you couldn't ask him anything," LaPoint said. "You'd say, 'Joaquin, how you feeling?' and he'd answer, 'Me one tough Dominican.'"

Andujar was able to start, and early in the game he told his teammates in the dugout, "You get me one run, we world champs."

The Cardinals scored in the bottom of the fourth, but in the fifth, Milwaukee tied the game. As time was called, Ken Oberkfell, playing third base, walked over to Andujar on the mound.

"I said, 'What do you think now?'" Oberkfell said. "He said, 'I think we need two.'"

Luckily, the Cardinals got more than enough runs, and Andujar's second victory in the Series was secured, along with the world championship, by closer Bruce Sutter.

"Sure, I was confident in my teammates and in myself," Andujar said.

Andujar has nothing but good things to say about his years in St. Louis and his teammates.

"I remember all the good times I had in St. Louis," Andujar said. "I remember all of those guys. George Hendrick, Ozzie Smith, Lonnie Smith, Tommy Herr, Willie McGee. I love those guys.

"We were close. The best friends I have in baseball [were] there. We won a championship, won the pennant. It was good times."

He called Ozzie Smith "the best I have seen on the infield" and called the Cardinals' defense "the best." "They never missed a ball. I throw what I want because I knew if [the batter] hit it, somebody [would] catch it."

While few of today's major league pitchers can reach the 200-inning plateau in a season, Andujar posted an amazing 265 innings pitched in 1982. The next three seasons with the Cardinals he registered 225, 261, and 269 innings, respectively.

After his stellar world championship season in 1982, things took a turn for the worse for Andujar in 1983. His record plummeted to 6–16 with a 4.16 ERA, but he was able to rebound the following year. Andujar was 20–14 with a 3.34 ERA with 12 complete games in 1984, finishing first in the National League in wins and strikeouts, and his four shutouts were also a league high. He also won his only Gold Glove that season. He finished fourth in the Cy Young Award balloting behind Rick Sutcliffe (16–1), Dwight Gooden (17–9), and his teammate Bruce Sutter (45 saves). He finished in the top 10 in walks/hits ratio (second), hits allowed per nine innings (fifth), complete games (second), fewest home runs allowed (seventh), and fewest hits (ninth).

Andujar never had a problem with bringing a pitch in high and tight—and if a batter had early success against Andujar in a game, chances are he would be knocked down later.

The following year brought another National League Championship to St. Louis, and Andujar again was a big reason why, following up his 20-win season by winning 21 games with a 3.40 ERA. He also kept his team laughing anytime he came up to bat.

Even though he never hit .200 in a season, Andujar was a switch-hitter. He would often bat from the left and right side against the same pitcher during different at-bats. The only thing stopping him from switching in the middle of an at-bat was the major league rule book.

After getting two hits in a game he was asked what pitches he would throw to himself.

"Fastball right down the middle," Andujar responded. "What do you think, I'd try to get myself out?"

The good times were rolling in 1985; however, by the end of the 1985 season, Andujar's arm was obviously worn out. He was 0–2 in the postseason that year with an ERA just less than nine runs a game.

That includes the infamous Game 7 relief appearance meltdown against the Kansas City Royals.

Herzog brought in Andujar to pitch in the fifth inning. Umpire Don Denkinger was working behind the plate—the night after blowing the call at first base that helped propel Kansas City to a dramatic Game 6 victory. (In the bottom of the ninth, with the Cardinals leading 1–0, Denkinger ruled Royals' pinch-hitter Jorge Orta safe at first on a play that replay cameras clearly show was an out. This opened the door to the Royals scoring the tying and winning runs moments later.)

Andujar, and Herzog, didn't make it out of the inning, both getting ejected for arguing ball-strike calls. The Royals eventually won 11–0.

That less-than-glamorous exit on October 28, 1985, turned out to be Andujar's final appearance in a Cardinals uniform.

About two weeks earlier, as Game 6 of the NLCS moved to the bottom of the ninth inning following Jack Clark's three-run, pennant-clinching home run against the Los Angeles Dodgers, Andujar had approached Herzog on the top step of the dugout.

Some say he pleaded with Herzog not to trade him.

"I told him how much I wanted to play for him," Andujar said.

Under orders from the top officials at Anheuser-Busch, the Cardinals' owners, Andujar was traded to Oakland over the winter for catcher Mike Heath.

"I was very disappointed, but I was a major leaguer. I moved on," Andujar said.

He won 12 games for an Oakland team that finished 10 games under .500 in 1986, but he was nearing the end of his career. He was hurt in most of 1987, and after returning to Houston in 1988, he won only two games before retiring.

"Age. The age don't let you play no more," he said.

Before his retirement, Andujar became one of the most entertaining players in baseball. He was always good for a great quote, joining such legendary wordsmiths as Yogi Berra and Casey Stengel. Here are some of his most famous sayings, which people remember to this day:

- "There is one word in America that says it all, and that one word is, 'You never know.'"
- "I throw the ball 92 miles an hour, but they hit it back just as hard."
- "There are 300,000 sportswriters, and they're all against me. Every one of them."
- "You can't worry if it's cold; you can't worry if it's hot; you only worry if you get sick. Because then if you don't get well, you die."
- "God is back in the National League. In fact, he's staying at my house. I'm having a barbecue for him."

Andujar still holds a warm spot in his heart for St. Louis and its fans.

"Anybody who knows me, knows I love St. Louis," he said. "The fans there are special."

So too is Herzog, in Andujar's eyes.

"Whitey—he is just great," Andujar said. "He was my daddy. He is a special man."

2 | Bob Forsch

The flight home from Milwaukee to St. Louis was not a good one for Bob Forsch following Game 5 of the 1982 World Series.

The Cardinals trailed the Series 3–2 and, along with his baggage, Forsch was dragging two of those losses and a 4.97 World Series ERA back to Busch Stadium. Forsch had pitched what he calls "my best game ever" in Game 1 of the National League Championship Series against Atlanta on October 7. He struck out six Braves, gave up just three hits, and won 7–0; however, he was hit hard and often during the Brewers' 10–0 win in Game 1 of the World Series.

"I don't know what the rest of the team felt, but I felt bad. I'm 0–2 in the World Series, and I hadn't pitched very well," Forsch said.

The camaraderie of that 1982 team then changed the mood on the airplane and possibly the outcome of the seven-game series.

"Bruce Sutter yells out, 'Party at the Forsches',' " Forsch said. "I said, 'Bruce, I don't think this is the time.' "

But Sutter was insistent, in part because "we had a finished basement," Forsch said. "I don't think so," said Forsch.

"Well, that's what we're doing," the stubborn Sutter said. "We're coming over."

Forsch said many of his Cardinals teammates met at his house later that evening and proceeded "to get plenty drunk. We didn't have a workout the next day, so we had a good time."

Forsch still resides in the St. Louis area, is tall and trim, and looks as if he could take the mound at any time. Since he retired in 1989, Forsch says calmly, "actually, I haven't worked."

He's a staple at St. Louis Cardinals fantasy camps, but he has no aspiration to return to baseball as a coach or manager. He's content being a baseball fan, golfing, and fishing.

"It was hard watching the guys leave for spring training the first couple of years I was out of baseball," he said. "They were going where it was warm, and I was stuck here in the cold. But then I would think, 'This is the third day of spring training. Boy, would I be sore right now.' I didn't miss it as much."

During the last years of his career, Forsch said, he contemplated staying in baseball after his retirement as either a coach or manager.

"Managing? Yes, I think I could do it. When I got out of baseball I was tired of traveling. I was tired of putting on my uniform in the summertime. I signed out of high school in 1968, and, with the exception of two strike years, I didn't have a summer vacation. It was nice to be able to not go on the field every day at 5:00 P.M.," Forsch said.

Forsch did actually have a stint at coaching, an experience he enjoyed.

"I helped out at John Burroughs [a private school in the St. Louis area] when my daughters [Amy and Kristin] were there, and I helped coach seventh- and eighth-grade girls basketball. I was the good guy. Peter Fischer was the head coach. He would make them cry, and I would go and console them," Forsch said with a smile.

Forsch also assisted the baseball team, which was constructed differently from most prep baseball teams.

"I really enjoyed it, especially because at Burroughs all students had to go out for a sport," he said. "Some would pick baseball, so you were faced with coaching some students who did not play baseball. I grew up playing baseball all summer; I wonder why kids don't do it anymore."

Forsch said if he had pursued the idea of becoming a manager, he had the best role model a ballplayer could have had.

"From the moment Whitey Herzog came over here, he was a winner. He had teams in Kansas City that didn't have the most talent, but everybody played hard and they won. People who didn't work, or were questionable in the clubhouse attitudewise, he cleaned them all out," Forsch said.

Shortly after Herzog arrived in St. Louis, and before he had general manager responsibilities, he approached free-agent-to-be Forsch on the field before a game and asked if he was playing without a contract for the next season.

"Does that bother you?" Forsch said Herzog asked him.

"I said no, and he wanted to know why. I told him that's the way they've always done it here. Whitey said 'I'll talk to some people,' and it was not too long after that that I signed the new contract.

"Whitey cared that much for all his players. He treated all people the same, not just the marquee people. He would talk to the 24th and 25th man on the team and ask about their families. He would say, 'You don't have to stroke the regular players, they read about themselves in the newspaper. The guys that fill in and get the key hits in timely situations are bench players, and you have to keep them happy too.'"

Forsch said Whitey also had a unique way of keeping the front office happy, especially the late August Busch Jr.

"He assessed what we had, knew what we needed, and he had such a good relationship with Mr. Busch that he could talk to him and make things happen. He could get a player here or there and still keep the overall salary picture the same," Forsch said.

Forsch said Herzog had an uncanny way of positioning the defense behind him based upon where opposing batters hit the ball against him. Once, Forsch decided to go it on his own against a hitter he had struggled with, and it resulted in a meeting with the manager.

"He called me in and asked, 'What's the story?' I told him I had been having trouble getting that guy out, so I decided to do something different. All he said was to let him know next time I was going to do something like that so he could compensate. He had it all figured out," Forsch said.

Forsch is one of many 1982 Cardinals who said the team's fortunes changed for the positive immediately upon Herzog's arrival at Busch Stadium, and the team actually had the best overall record in the NL East in 1981. However, because of the strike, the season was divided into halves and the Cardinals finished in second place in the NL East both times. There was no postseason baseball in St. Louis in 1981, but the stage was set for 1982.

"We knew we had a good baseball team; the expectations were high when we entered the season," Forsch said. "We didn't get off to a quick start, but things came together pretty quickly. Whenever we had an injury, somebody stepped up and filled in. It was just one of those things where everything fell into place."

Herzog also brought a happy clubhouse with him, and soon the team's antics kept each other in a lighthearted mood—regardless of what transpired on the field that day.

By the All-Star break Forsch, who finished 15–9 with a sparkling 3.48 ERA, said he remained confident in the team, even though it lacked power and runs were sometimes hard to come by.

"You knew if you got three or four runs you better make it hold up," he said. "While we lacked power, we did have Sutter in the bullpen and great defense."

Things kept falling into place for the Cardinals through the NLCS, and then everything fell apart for Forsch and the Cardinals during the Game 1 World Series debacle.

"I had been watching the American League [Championship] Series because my brother Ken was pitching for the California Angels and they were playing the Brewers. Their series also went five games, but the Angels lost. If they had won, my brother was in line to pitch Game 1. I guess it was a blessing they lost," Forsch said.

"We had advance scouts who went out and put together these reports on the Brewers—pitch this guy here, this guy is slow, pitch this way in this situation. Well, we pitched that way and it seemed like every base hit was a foot from somebody. The slow guys were beating out hits by a step. When the game was over, I remember Tommy Herr, Ozzie Smith, and a few others getting together and basically saying screw those reports and play the way we've played everyone else all season long. We went back to pitching to our strengths instead of the batters' weaknesses."

After winning Game 2 in St. Louis on a Wednesday night, the Cardinals and Brewers played Game 3 on a chilly Friday night in Milwaukee.

That was the night Willie McGee would forever become a part of baseball history.

"I pitched a lot of 'B' games in spring training, so I saw Willie play down there. He had a world of talent but was unorthodox. He would swing at terrible pitches, then you would throw the same bad pitch and he would rake it someplace," Forsch said of his first encounters with the skinny kid who came over in a trade from the New York Yankees.

"He did it all so humbly, like he was embarrassed. When he came up, I knew he wouldn't hurt us. He just kept putting up great numbers, and doing it quietly."

McGee's bat and glove were anything but quiet in that Game 3. Two home runs and a home-run-saving over-the-wall snatch on a drive by Brewers outfielder Gorman Thomas late in the game thrilled the nation.

"Ozzie had taken Willie under his wing, and that made him a better ballplayer," Forsch said. "Willie was open to suggestion; he listened. He wasn't like many of the young players today who think they already know it all."

The Cardinals dropped the next two games, including Sunday's 6–4 loss that Forsch pitched, and the flight home and party at the Forsches' followed.

Game 6 was payback for the Cardinals as they blasted Milwaukee 13–1 behind a complete-game effort by John Stuper.

"I never had so much fun playing cards as I did during that long rain delay," Forsch said. He had no doubt that there would be a seventh game.

Then came Game 7. Forsch said because of the off day on Monday and Stuper's masterful performance, all the bullpen was rested, and he saw no chance of pitching that night.

"I just had to sit and watch. I was on every pitch," he said.

When his buddy Sutter struck out Gorman Thomas in the ninth inning, Forsch said he can't remember whom he hugged first or what he did exactly.

"We ran on the field and just started jumping on each other," he said. He later shared some champagne with his parents and relatives, calling it "special to have my dad there."

Forsch, who beams when talking about the championship season, said the World Series victory was more precious than either of his no-hitters because "it was a total team effort, and it takes an entire season to accomplish, going all the way back to spring training.

"A lot of a no-hitter is luck. It's just one game, and then it is gone away. It takes an entire team to win the World Series. No player plays every day, no pitcher pitches every day. It is really a team effort." Forsch and the Cardinals were in contention again in 1983 but came up short in the NL East race. In 1984, Forsch had surgery and did not pitch until the final month of the season.

"That went well, so I knew I would be ready for 1985," Forsch said.

Forsch lost the fifth game of the 1985 World Series, and the Kansas City Royals prevailed in a controversial seven-game series that included Don Denkinger's infamous call at first base in the ninth inning of Game 6.

"Even when we lost the World Series, the fans of St. Louis didn't get down on us. They wouldn't get down on us when we didn't win during a season. There was a 'We'll get them next year' attitude," Forsch said.

Following the 1987 World Series loss to the Minnesota Twins, Forsch was traded to the Houston Astros.

"It was tough. I missed the atmosphere," Forsch said of his new surroundings. "I grew up a Cardinal; it was the only organization I knew. I knew not only the people on the field, but the people who worked at the stadium and in the team offices."

When he arrived in Houston, Forsch said, it was odd to be with a new organization, "although at the time I thought I might get back into baseball [after retiring] so it was an opportunity to see how an organization different from St. Louis' was run."

He called his first trip back to St. Louis as an Astro "weird."

"I wanted to do well. I didn't want to embarrass myself. As I remember, I pitched here once and gave up two home runs," he said.

The Cardinals honored Forsch before a game and presented him with several gifts, including a clock.

"I was treated well by the fans, and that kind of stuff embarrasses me, though."

The Astros were in the NL West race in 1989 and came close but didn't prevail.

"The fans were totally different," Forsch said. "In St. Louis, the fans expected us to win. There, it seemed like they were expecting us to lose. It was a much different atmosphere; it was mind-boggling. It was really hard to figure out."

Neither the fans nor the media were too intrusive during his playing days, something else that made St. Louis a special place to play.

"It wasn't like playing in New York or Los Angeles where everybody is looking for a scoop and there are so many media people. We didn't have the people standing outside conversations, writing what they think they heard. We didn't have any of that," he said.

During the 1989 season, Forsch said, he made up his mind to end his playing career.

"I probably could have kicked around from team to team," he said. "I didn't feel I was pitching as well as I could. The losses were harder to handle, as was not pitching well and getting no decisions. There just comes a time when you don't play up to your own expectation and it's time to leave. I was backing up third too many times; it was time to quit."

Forsch said he was "blessed" to win a World Series, win three National League titles, pitch two no-hitters, and hit a grand slam. "I even came in a game and saved it for Bruce Sutter [in 1982]."

But he doesn't want to step on the mound for old-time's sake.

"My arm hurts when I throw now. If anything, I'd rather be able to go hit than pitch. That might be fun," said Forsch, who won a *Sporting News* Silver Bat in 1980 for his hitting prowess.

Forsch said he still roots for the Cardinals, although he admits he's a "front-runner fan."

"I want them to do well because a lot of my friends still work [for the Cardinals]," he said. "I want the whole organization to do well. Plus, it's just so much fun to go to playoff games. When you are playing, you get to the stadium before the crowd and you leave after it is gone. Now, I can have a couple of beers before the game just like the other fans."

Forsch, Ozzie Smith, and David Green are the last of the 1982 Cardinals that reside in St. Louis, although several players from the 1985 and 1987 NL Champion Cardinals remain in the area.

"I like to wear that 1982 ring around them," Forsch said. "It's special. I get a pleasure out of wearing it because it's only Ozzie, David, and I that have one."

3 | David Green

Ask any Cardinals fan which players from the 1982 team still reside in the St. Louis area. The answer almost assuredly will be "two—Ozzie Smith and Bob Forsch."

That answer is incorrect.

David Green is alive and well and living in the metropolitan area. He was part of the Winter Warm-Up celebration at the St. Louis Millennium Hotel in January 2002, has a relationship with former Cardinal and Hall of Famer Lou Brock and former Redbird Curt Ford, and is a kids' baseball camp barnstormer.

He also has one of the most interesting jobs that a former major league player could aspire to—he helps operate a dog-grooming business on the south side of the city of St. Louis.

While Green battled with substance abuse during his career and faced serious charges following a car accident in which one of his passengers was killed, his life has not gone to the dogs.

He does seem a bit hesitant to speak about his current life, and it was almost impossible to pin him down for an interview.

"I'm doing fine. My life is good. I'm just very busy these days," Green said.

David Alejandro "Casaya" Green was born December 4, 1960, in Managua, Nicaragua, and made his major league debut with the Cardinals on September 4, 1981. The Cardinals had acquired him from the Brewers in the deal that sent Ted Simmons to Milwaukee.

He entered the league as a hard-hitting outfield and first-base prospect who stood at 6'3", 170 pounds. He had a football player's build, but his body fell victim to injury and substance abuse.

"When you look back at phenoms, and in their day, if you saw David Green and Darryl Strawberry standing together in baseball uniforms, you would say that they just looked like baseball players before you ever saw them move," Whitey Herzog said. "They had potential, but both of them never reached it."

Green was the Cardinals' starting center fielder when the 1982 season opened, but he struggled early in the year and then had to go on the disabled list in May when he pulled a hamstring muscle. That opened a spot for Willie McGee to be called up from Louisville, and even though Green was expected to regain the job as soon as he was healthy, McGee played so well that it was almost impossible for him to come out of the lineup.

Green finished the regular season with a .283 average in 76 games, hitting two homers and driving in 23 runs. He also stole 11 bases. He got a hit in the playoff series against Atlanta, then appeared in all seven games in the World Series against Milwaukee. He had two hits in 10 plate appearances with a walk. He scored three runs and sparked two Cardinals rallies with a double and a triple, respectively.

In 1983 Green's progress continued. He played in 146 games, hit .284, and had eight home runs and 69 RBIs. He still was a feared base stealer, collecting 34 steals. He was third in the NL in triples with 10.

The next season, 1984, he hit 15 home runs—which was outstanding becaise Busch Stadium's walls had not yet been moved in —with 65 RBI. He stole 17 bases, but his average dipped to .268 and

Image by Lew Portnoy, Spectra-Action Inc.

Ozzie Smith's back flips became a tradition, and a moment all Cardinals fans enjoyed.

Darrell Porter was one of those special players whose most important skill was being a winner.

Image by Lew Portnoy, Spectra-Action Inc.

Bob Forsch, one of the anchors of the rotation, tied for the team lead with 15 victories in the 1982 regular season.

Image by Lew Portnoy, Spectra-Action Inc.

Image by Lew Portnoy, Spectra-Action Inc.

Jeff Lahti was an important setup man, helping bridge the gap between the starters and Bruce Sutter.

Image by Lew Portnoy, Spectra-Action Inc.

Tito Landrum contributed in many ways to the Cardinals' success in 1982, as well as in later years.

Image by Lew Portnoy, Spectra-Action Inc.

"Silent" George Hendrick let his bat do all the talking for him—he never spoke with the media.

Image by Lew Portnoy, Spectra-Action Inc.

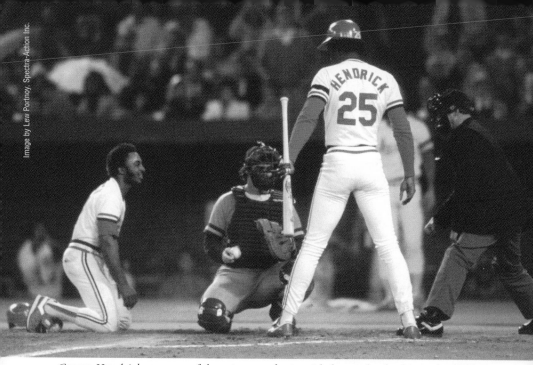

George Hendrick was one of the veterans who provided great leadership to the 1982 team.

Image by Lew Portnoy, Spectra-Action Inc.

Lonnie Smith was always an exciting player, especially when he was running the bases.

Image by Lew Portnoy, Spectra-Action Inc.

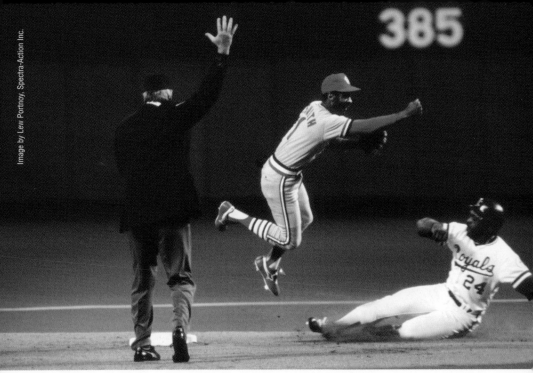

Ozzie Smith was an acrobat on defense, making plays others could only dream about.

Image by Lew Portnoy, Spectra-Action Inc.

David Green showed a lot of promise as a young player, but personal problems would keep him from achieving his potential.

Coming off the bench and delivering a clutch pinch-hit was Steve Braun's role with the Cardinals for years.

Image by Lew Portnoy, Spectra-Action Inc.

Glenn Brummer kept everybody on the team loose and, even though he didn't catch much, he played well when called upon.

Image by Lew Portnoy, Spectra-Action Inc.

John Stuper's performance in Game 6 of the World Series guaranteed that the Series would reach a seventh game.

Image by Lew Portnoy, Spectra-Action Inc.

he struck out an appalling 105 times. He ranked eighth in National League strikeouts that season.

During the 1984 off-season he was traded to San Francisco in the deal that brought Jack Clark to St. Louis. During his only season in San Francisco, he played in 106 games, hit .248, and registered five home runs and 20 RBIs.

Green returned to St. Louis for part of the 1987 season, but he was not with the team in the World Series. He played in just 14 games.

Although his struggles with alcohol no doubt were among the factors in his disappointing career, Green has continued to keep baseball a part of his life.

Green took part in the Cardinals annual Winter Warm-Up in January 2002 and signed autographs and interacted with fans. The Warm-Up is not just a weekend autograph show. Thousands of devoted Cardinals fans pack the hotel ballroom, and dozens of former Cardinals greats are invited to participate.

He is also not a stranger to his old place of employment, Busch Stadium.

Green attends games occasionally and can be spotted around the clubhouse. He was at Opening Day a year ago, and he also was on hand when the Barry Bonds show came to St. Louis in 2001.

Green spent the pregame hour with Giants coach Tommy McGraw; he had obviously developed friendships during the season he spent in San Francisco after he was dealt from St. Louis.

"A great season," is how Green described the World Series 1982 season.

Then he was off the phone and out the door on the way to Louisiana, Missouri, for one of the baseball camps he attends. Louisiana is a small town just south of Hannibal, Missouri. It's Mark Twain territory—far from the bright lights of major league stadiums.

Clancy Boyer, who is a friend of Hall of Famer Lou Brock, organizes the annual camp. He is president and CEO of Clancy Boyer Chevrolet Pontiac & Buick Inc. in Louisiana, one of the largest dealerships in the area.

The town's best diamond, Wallace Field, is where the camp is held, and David Green is welcome.

He has left a lasting positive impression on the youths he works with and the adults that help make the camp a reality.

"He is a super guy," says Susan Merkel, an account manager with the city of Louisiana. She works with the annual baseball camp. "He's really good with the kids. They are really impressed with him."

Former Cardinal Curt Ford also took part in the camp, which draws between 20 and 30 players from the small rural town.

"[David] was here last year, and they made a point of inviting him back," Merkel said. "He just does a great job."

This year's camp was scheduled for April 27, but heavy downpours led to its postponement.

Green and company made the 90-minute drive for naught—but returned a week later and the camp was held.

The grooming shop where Green helps many of St. Louis' finest canines look their best is located just off Jefferson at Utah. It's not the most affluent part of the city, but it has one of the south side's most active small business communities. It is also one of the more diverse areas of St. Louis, which, like many American cities, is racially polarized when it comes to residency.

It might look like an odd place for a dog-grooming shop, but Green said it's doing good business.

"It is a very busy time for [early spring]," he said. "I'm sorry I don't have time to speak with you. It's just I've been busy."

The fact that Green is busy is good news for Cardinals fans.

4 | George Hendrick

Twenty years later, "Silent" George Hendrick is still silent.

Hendrick was in his first season of managing in 2002, directing the California League Class A Lake Elsinore Storm, an affiliate of the San Diego Padres. But neither his new position nor the span of two decades has changed Hendrick's viewpoint on speaking with the media regarding himself and his tenure with the Cardinals.

As was the case during his playing career, talking with people who work for him and who are around him on a daily basis, you get the picture of a jovial man with a quick wit and a kind heart. He is defined by those who know him as a man who understands and appreciates the nuances of baseball, and also of society.

He's a positive man with an interesting story to tell—but he won't share his story with anyone other than his players. He is still resistant to speaking with media representatives, including even the beat writers who cover the Storm. That was the same position he took during most of his playing career and during his two years as the Cardinals' hitting coach in 1996 and 1997.

Considering one of a manager's usual responsibilities is to have daily contact with reporters, this puts both Hendrick and the beat reporters assigned to his team in a rather unusual position.

"He was real standoffish at first," said Greg Bell, a sports reporter with *The Californian* who covers the team. "Early in the season I asked him about a player's injury; he said, 'Go ask the trainer.' I asked him about a player's hitting; he said, 'Go ask Rob Deer.'"

Deer, also a former major league standout with the Detroit Tigers, is the Storm hitting coach, and he coaches first base while Hendrick directs his team from the third-base box. Hendrick is also assisted by pitching coach Mike Harkey, another major league veteran. Deer served as hitting coach for Single A Eugene last season, and Harkey was the pitching coach for Ft. Wayne.

While he is tight with his team and coaches, Hendrick has just begun to build relationships with media members.

Another writer from *The Californian,* Adrian Pomeray, said, "You're fine as long as you talk about the team and the game."

Hendrick, who declined a specific request for an interview to talk about his career and the 1982 season in particular for this book, was not bitter or mean. Hendrick just doesn't wish to speak with the media. It dates back to before he became a member of the St. Louis Cardinals.

Hendrick became a media recluse during his time with the Cleveland Indians. A reported flare-up between him and manager Ken Aspromonte led to Hendrick's taking a vow of silence, one that he refused to waiver from for the remainder of his career.

"George would talk all the time," said 1982 teammate Bob Forsch. "He just wouldn't talk on the record. I remember he and [*St. Louis Post-Dispatch* Cardinals beat writer] Rick Hummel would talk all the time, especially about basketball. That's George's game."

Andy Van Slyke broke into the majors with St. Louis during Hendrick's final season as a Cardinal, 1984. Hendrick still manned right field, and Van Slyke platooned at third base. Van Slyke recalled an episode in Cincinnati.

"I was on deck, and Mario Soto was throwing a no-hitter against us. He had George down two strikes, and he had him. George didn't have a chance. For some reason, Soto decided to knock George down. He threw a pitch between his head and batting helmet. So George got up, dusted himself off—in his slow, cool way, no hurry. The next pitch, George hit into the left-center-field seats. The score was now 1–1; there goes the no-hitter.

"George loped around the bases real slow, and about five steps from the plate he actually started to walk. He didn't say anything to the pitcher, didn't show him up."

Van Slyke makes his voice raise to a shrill tone when he finishes the story. "George said, 'I was going to let him go. I was just going to take that last one. But he ticked me off.'"

Hendrick reportedly has a stockpile of stories that he shares with his team—even though many of his players were either newborns or toddlers during the 1982 World Series.

The Lake Elsinore Storm was the Baseball America Minor League Baseball Team of the Year during a Cal League championship season in 2001. General Manager David Oster was named 2001 Executive of the Year by the California League, and he created this opportunity for Hendrick, one of few African-American managers at any level of baseball.

The Storm got off to a slow start in 2002. In an early season four-game series with Lancaster, Hendrick watched his team held hitless into the seventh inning. A late rally fell short, and the team lost 2–1.

Hendrick clapped and encouraged his team throughout the evening. The weak offensive effort didn't dim Hendrick's spirit about his team or its potential.

His postgame comments also offered insight into his philosophy of the game.

"When you face a good pitcher with good stuff, that's what is going to happen. Good pitching stops good hitting. You've got to tip your hat to the pitcher. He threw a great game," Hendrick said in a short conversation following the game.

His team had two pitching gems in succession thrown at it, and Hendrick remained confident.

"That's part of the life of baseball, man. Sometimes you face two or three good [pitchers] in a row. This is a good experience for these guys.

"These guys will hit. I'm not terribly concerned. They just made the jump from short season last year so it's going to take a minute for them to figure out that they belong here. But they'll figure it out pretty quick."

The confidence and enthusiasm immediately brushed off on Hendrick's team, a collaboration of players ranging from their late teens to late twenties.

"He's most definitely interesting. He keeps the whole team loose," according to pitcher Bryan Gall. "The best thing about him is listening to his stories. He tells one every day, it's something new. There's a story about everything."

Gall continued, saying, "He is a really good guy to play for. He basically just asks us to go out and play hard every day and give it all we have. As long as we don't show him up, he won't show us up. As a pitcher, I like listening to him get on hitters about not taking the right approach. I love the guy."

Catcher Andre Gomez kept repeating one word when it came to his manager: "awesome."

"The guy is awesome. He's the easiest guy to talk to; it's all positive. When we're struggling, he looks at the bright side and tries to turn it around. He gets into positive thinking," Gomez said. "How can you not learn from him? He was in the bigs for 18 years."

Unlike most major leaguers who played for that duration, Hendrick has decided to return to his roots in minor league baseball. Hendrick was born in Los Angeles in 1949 and starred in basketball and baseball as a youth. While he spent decades traveling first class, lodging in the finest establishments, and dining at the best restaurants, he has returned to bus travel, fast-food meals, and budget motels while on the road.

Lake Elsinore has just three hotels, and a tourist could eat his or her way through its restaurants in about two weeks. One of the hotels has a casino that boasts "no bust" blackjack and other games. The hotel and casino is an official sponsor of the Storm. It is also the official hangout of Storm players after a game. Following the 2–1 loss, several players met there for loud talk, dozens of cell phone calls, and beer drinking.

Although the season was just a few weeks old, the bartenders knew the players, as did many of the bar's other customers. The party went well past midnight. Some players spoke of sleeping in the next day, while others had an 8:30 A.M. tee time at a nearby golf course.

Just 11 miles down the highway sits Temecula, a larger city with more people and more to do—but the Storm players looked relaxed and at home at the hotel/casino, which could be best described as "Spartan."

Lake Elsinore is a throwback compared to sprawling San Diego and Los Angeles. In a nostalgic twist, on select Saturdays during the spring and summer, Main Street is closed to all cars other than classic models. The store owners and operators along Main Street play music from the fifties, and the town becomes an official "cruising" strip. It draws visitors from throughout California.

In addition to the town's southwestern culture and beautiful scenery, the Storm stands out as the jewel of the town.

In this town, Hendrick has quickly become a favorite of local fans and staff members who work at The Diamond.

"He's a great guy," said Mary Jane Langton, assistant supervisor of security at the pristine stadium.

One of Langton's duties is patrolling the player/season-ticket-holder parking lot before games.

"He always asks if I need anything when he pulls in," she said. "He'll always offer to get us water. He's always smiling."

The water offer means a lot in the desert. Sometimes, games begin with the thermometer well above the 100-degree mark. However, during the Lancaster series in late April, not only did it rain in Southern California, it poured. The temperature also dipped into the high 40s during two games.

The inclement weather and the team's sub-.500 start didn't dampen Hendrick's nonstop enthusiasm, nor did it seem to bother the Californians in attendance.

A Storm game is a family event. Children roll and tumble down a grass slope adjacent to right field, and there is some type of activity during every half inning. There are video games and other activities in the concourse for children as well.

The stadium sports a "green monster"–type wall that is actually taller than Fenway Park's in Boston. The right-field foul pole is a scant 320 feet away, but it takes a bit of a drive to clear the ad-covered wall.

It doesn't appear to have taken Hendrick, who also managed in the Arizona Fall League, long to remember that baseball at this level is a lot different than in the major leagues.

Tom Davey, a Padres Triple A pitching prospect, was assigned to Lake Elsinore for five appearances. Although Hendrick wants to win every game and demands 100 percent effort from his team, the overall organization must come first.

Davey started two straight games for the Storm, pitching one inning each time. The other youthful pitchers had to wait. Hendrick didn't seem to mind.

He didn't seem fazed when his team was being shut out and no hit—and he showed no emotion when the team scored just one run after loading the bases with no outs in the eighth inning on the way to the 2–1 loss.

He had seen it all during his brief minor league playing career and during 18 years in the major leagues.

During that 18-year career, Hendrick was a four-time All-Star including two times for the Indians. He was named one of the team's all-time top 100 players. He also was a teammate of baseball's first black manager, Frank Robinson, when Robinson played and managed for Cleveland.

He was an All-Star with the Cardinals in 1980 and 1983. That 1980 season was one of the most productive of his lengthy career, with 25 home runs and 109 RBIs.

While his nontalking status might be his legacy in St. Louis, history will also remember that he was responsible for the most important base hit of the 1982 season.

After falling behind 3–1 in the top of the sixth inning of the seventh game of the World Series, the Cardinals came up with three runs in the bottom of the inning. After Keith Hernandez tied the game with a two-run single, Hendrick slapped a textbook single through the right side of the Brewers' infield off reliever Bob McClure. The Cardinals added a pair of insurance runs in the eighth to win 6–3.

Hendrick hit .321, scored five runs, and had five RBIs in the seven-game showdown.

"He really didn't have raw power," manager Whitey Herzog said. "But our stadium at the time didn't feature a lot of home runs. George always hit from 19 to 22 home runs, he'd drive in around 90, and he was a Gold Glove–caliber right fielder.

"I had never met George when I first came to St. Louis. In my first week as manager here he didn't run a ball out. We talked about it, and he said it wouldn't happen again and it didn't. He really became a good guy in the clubhouse along with everything else."

Hendrick was indeed a favorite of his teammates.

"George kept everybody loose. When things were tight, George was calm. It helped us all just stay relaxed," Forsch said.

Hendrick broke into the big leagues with the Oakland A's in 1971 and played in his first World Series during the 1972 season.

Oakland surprised the powerful Cincinnati Reds, although Hendrick was not much help. He hit .133 in five games during that Series. He was traded to St. Louis from San Diego after 36 games of the 1978 season, and he played with the Cardinals through 1984. His playing career ended with the California Angels in 1988.

Hendrick returned to St. Louis as batting coach in 1996 and 1997. He was the first in what became a revolving door of hitting instructors for manager Tony LaRussa that has included Dave Parker, Mike Easler, and Mitchell Page. The Cardinals advanced to the seventh game of the National League Championship Series before falling to the Atlanta Braves in 1996.

In the request for an interview for this book, Hendrick was asked at what point in his career did he think he would like to manage. Because the answer involved his speaking about himself, he declined to answer. When it comes to Hendrick, even the simplest inquiry is quite complex.

"I was interviewing him, and the topic of losing came up. He said, 'I've been on teams that lost 100 games.' Then he said, 'Wait, I want to say I've seen teams lose 100 games,'" Bell said.

Even though he is a minor league manager, there is very little about Hendrick's new place of employment that is minor league.

The Diamond seats about 8,000, and fans have a scenic view of a mountain range over the outfield walls. It opened in 1994, and the city of just under 35,000 residents soon landed a California League franchise.

The stadium's green roofs and classic southwestern style make it one of the most impressive structures in Lake Elsinore. Any minor league team would be proud to call The Diamond its home.

Although Hendrick has aged since his St. Louis years, he still has the graceful stride that carried him to fly balls. He also still wears his baseball pants all the way down to his spikes. The no-stirrup look is now a fashion craze throughout baseball, and it was Hendrick that first wore his pants with such flair.

He does not sport the "natural" that was the most popular hairstyle of black Americans during his heyday, but he still has some wave and curl in his hair. His smile is bright and engaging.

Hendrick looks as if he can also grab a bat and still belt a 90-mph fastball. His body is toned, and he has not gained much weight since his retirement more than a decade ago.

He always looked the part of a basketball player, and he still retains an interest in the game.

Before a postgame interview following a game against Lancaster, Hendrick sneaked a quick peek at a training room television to catch a few seconds of the Los Angeles Lakers dismantling the Portland Trailblazers in an NBA playoff game.

His son, Brian, was a star guard with the University of California, and he scored 13 points in a 1990 upset victory over Bobby Knight's Indiana Hoosiers in the first round of the NCAA tournament. Connecticut blew out his team in the second-round game, but Hendrick scored 12 points. Three years later, the younger Hendrick again helped lead his team to the NCAA tournament before bowing out 93–76 to Kansas in the Midwest Regional semifinal. The game was played in—of all places—St. Louis. Hendrick scored 15 points in the contest.

Hendrick also takes part in the annual Cardinals Legends Camp and is listed among players scheduled to return in 2003.

While he doesn't speak about his Cardinals days, it seems he can't escape them. During the series with Lancaster coaches and players from the Corona, California, Pony League attended a game. The team was the Cardinals, and the players were outfitted in jerseys with the traditional "birds on the bat" design.

During the first inning a Corona Cardinals player, a girl, kept leaning over the box seats railing and yelling toward Hendrick. It was in the middle of an inning, but the cool Hendrick took it in stride. Between batters, he walked over to the little girl and apparently told her he couldn't talk to her at that time, but that he would return.

After the inning, he returned to the little girl, answered her inquiry, and then disappeared into the dugout to watch his team play defense.

Hendrick has a lot to say to youthful fans, his up-and-coming players, and the Lake Elsinore Storm staff.

He just chooses to hush up when it comes to the media. With success comes additional responsibility, so as he rises through the minor league system, Hendrick might have to open up a bit more—but in the meantime, the moniker "Silent" George still fits.

5 | Keith Hernandez

Still a few months shy of his 49th birthday, Keith Hernandez is quite a bit younger than the typical snowbirds who migrate from New York to Florida in the winter. Like his fellow New Yorkers, however, escaping the city to spend some time in the sun in Jupiter, Florida, is an enjoyable part of his life.

Hernandez became a New Yorker against his will, leaving the Cardinals in a trade to the Mets on June 15, 1983. The announcement of the trade on the Busch Stadium message board was greeted with a resounding echo of boos, and downstairs in the Cardinals' locker room, Hernandez was on the telephone, calling his agent to find out if he could block the trade.

Even though he had been one of the stars of the 1982 World Series victory, collecting one of the key hits in Game 7—on his 29th birthday against childhood pal Bob McClure—Hernandez had known for some time that the Cardinals were trying to trade him. He did exercise a clause in his contract to block a deal to the Astros, but he had no such protection for the Mets.

"Thank God I didn't, because I probably would have blocked it," Hernandez said. "I could tell a trade was coming, because I knew I wasn't in Whitey's good graces. It was the trading deadline, and I remember telling Buddy Bates [the equipment manager] that I would be in another uniform tomorrow."

Herzog was bothered by Hernandez's attitude in 1983, and Hernandez admits he had reached a lull in his career at that point. He needed a spark to rejuvenate his career, and that came with the trade to the Mets. Herzog also was concerned that with Hernandez scheduled to become a free agent at the end of the 1983 season, the Cardinals would not get anything for him if he was not re-signed, and that was what he expected would happen.

Herzog was one of Hernandez's biggest boosters early in his St. Louis tenure. When he was originally deciding how to remake the Cardinals' lineup, one of his ideas was to move Hernandez to left field—despite his outstanding defensive ability at first—and move Ted Simmons to first. That plan fell apart when Simmons changed his mind about the position switch, forcing Herzog to deal Simmons to Milwaukee.

Simmons' decision actually allowed the Cardinals to form one of the best defensive infields ever, with Hernandez at first, Tom Herr at second, Ozzie Smith at short, and Ken Oberkfell at third.

"I'm not saying Keith was the best first baseman I've ever seen, but he was amongst them," Herzog said.

Herzog also has great praise for Hernandez's offensive performance during his years with the Cardinals.

"I still say that if Keith had not been so worried about his hitting he could have hit .400," Herzog said. "He never swung and missed the ball. Of all the people I managed, he and George Brett were the two best hit-and-run guys I've ever seen. Keith would come up to me before going to bat and say, 'Can I hit and run?' He always wanted to help me manage, but he was a very intelligent ballplayer."

With the benefit of 20 years of knowledge, Hernandez is able to put the trade in historical perspective. While he admits he would have preferred to play his entire career in St. Louis, it was best for his professional life that he went to the Mets. He and his wife, Sue, separated after the trade and later divorced, but Hernandez said that very likely would have happened even had he remained in St. Louis.

The hardest part of his move to New York was the separation from his three daughters, Jessie, Melissa, and Mary. "It was difficult not having them around, not being there," Hernandez said. "I wish I could have been there. I have a good relationship with them now, and I'm grateful for that."

At the time of the trade, Hernandez said he had no idea he would still be living in New York 20 years later, calling a 28th-floor apartment in midtown Manhattan home when he isn't at the townhouse in Jupiter, which he purchased in 1992.

"It was a city that I never went out in when I was with the Cardinals," Hernandez said. "I stayed in my room during the day and parked myself at the hotel bar after the game. But when I got to the Mets, Rusty Staub told me that if I was going to be single, I had to stay in the city and not live out on Long Island or in Connecticut. We had some other single guys on the team—Ed Lynch and Ron Darling—and we all stayed there. It took me about six weeks to realize how much the city had to offer."

Hernandez didn't know that he would soon be in for another dramatic change in his life, in spring training during the 1985 season, when he answered a phone call and found the FBI on the other end of the line. They were investigating the use of illegal drugs by major league players.

The use of recreational drugs by major leaguers was becoming a serious problem in the early eighties, and both baseball security officers and the FBI were investigating potential drug sources. Their investigation centered on Pittsburgh, where they found links to several of the athletes who reportedly were abusing drugs.

Several players were called as witnesses during the trials, including Hernandez. As a result of the investigations, seven drug dealers either pleaded guilty or were convicted of selling cocaine to players.

Hernandez was eventually granted immunity from prosecution in exchange for his testimony, and even though he avoided a prison sentence, he knew he would be forever scarred because of his association with the trial in Pittsburgh.

"It affected a lot of people," said Hernandez, as he took a sip from a bottle of water while sitting on a lounge chair on the deck of his townhouse. "It was one of the biggest mistakes of my life. I really felt bad for my girls and what they had to go through. I would come to St. Louis and get booed, and they had to sit in the stands and hear that. Melissa would be crying, and I am really regretful for what I put them through.

"It was just typical me. When I was a kid, my mom would say, 'Now you guys go out and play and don't go in the creek and get wet.' And of course we would all go in the creek, and I would follow my brother's steps and fall in the creek. My mom tanned my hide when I got home. That was just typical me, with impulsive behavior.

"A lot of people were monkeying around with drugs back then; it was just the thing to do, but that doesn't make it right. I thought that chapter of my life was behind me and that it was over, because I had quit, but then came the phone call from the FBI. It came back to haunt me."

Hernandez tried to turn that sad episode of his life into a positive by using his experiences to try to make sure other people, especially children, did not get involved with drugs.

"There is nothing good about it, and I can talk freely with kids about it," he said. "I talk to my friends' kids, but more importantly, to my kids. You are what you are. You do what you do. You make your own bed and you have to sleep in it. It's something I regret and I look back and kick myself in the butt."

Hernandez is at least grateful that he was able to stop his drug use on his own. He did not go to a rehab center, as did other players who became drug victims. He was a witness to more drug problems on the Mets, affecting players such as Dwight Gooden and Darryl Strawberry, problems that have continued even after their playing careers came to an end.

Hernandez's other regret was the way his baseball career ended. He enjoyed many good times with the Mets, including another World Series championship in 1986, but injuries began to catch up with him, and when his back went out while he was playing for Cleveland in 1990, he knew his career was over.

His father died of cancer the same year.

"My dad sawed off a Little League bat when I was five years old and started throwing tennis balls at the garage door," Hernandez said. "From then until I retired at age 38, I was very dedicated to baseball. It was ironic that he died my last year of baseball. It was like he was just there for my career and had nothing else to live for. My mom had died two years earlier. I told him I was going to retire, he found out he had cancer, and nine months later he was dead."

Partially because he did not like the way his career ended, Hernandez was able to begin his life after baseball without difficulty. He divorced himself from everything he had done while he played and didn't watch the game, even on television—not even the World Series—for five years. He quit smoking; he stopped doing crossword puzzles. He audited history classes at Columbia University—he had thoughts of earning a college degree but abandoned that goal when he found out one of the required classes was Spanish. One of his most enjoyable classes was English composition 101, having to write three-paragraph essays.

When he is in Florida, he is outdoors as much as possible. He co-owns a 23-foot boat and has kayaks on the floor of his garage. He watches a lot of college and pro football, but little other television. He enjoys the movies and going out to different events in New York. He doesn't flinch when people recognize him, but he likes being anonymous.

The most notoriety he received after his career ended came with a single appearance on the *Seinfeld* television show.

"Scott Boras was my last agent, and they called and asked if I would go out to Los Angeles and tape an episode of the show," Hernandez said. "It was the second year of the show, and I really didn't know much about it. I'm not much of a TV guy. Scott said, 'It's a comedy show. They'll fly you out to L.A. first class, put you up in a hotel for a week, and pay you $15,000.' I said sure, I'll do it.

"Little did I know it would turn out to be one of the more famous episodes of the show. It gave me exposure to a whole different group of people who had never seen me play."

Even though he liked the attention, Hernandez decided television and acting weren't for him. He didn't enjoy all of the waiting around that was involved, and one facet of his life that he has enjoyed the most since being out of baseball is that he doesn't have to be anywhere at any certain time and can set his own schedule as he pleases.

"Baseball was very good to me," Hernandez said. "I was able to do something I loved and get ahead in life. They are making tons of money today, but I can't say I didn't make any. The most I ever made in one year was $2 million, but it took a lot longer to get there. Luckily I was able to save."

Hernandez does not have many complimentary things to say about the game of baseball today and how it has changed not only from 20 years ago but also since he stopped playing. He laments how power and the desire for home runs has taken away some of the subtleties of the game that were so important in his era.

"It seems everybody's been told if they hit 25 or 30 home runs they are going to get an $80 million contract," he said. "You don't have guys trying to get the runner over. I saw a *USA Today* article that said nobody in baseball had a .400 on-base percentage last year. What's going on here? They don't want to walk; they want a maximum number of at-bats. It's just all power."

Hernandez will be back in baseball on a limited basis in 2002 for the first time since he retired, joining the television broadcast crew of the Mets. He will broadcast between 35 and 50 games, enough to keep him busy but still leave plenty of free time.

One concession to age is that Hernandez now needs reading glasses and has to use glasses when he is driving at night. Otherwise, he actually is in better shape than when he played.

"I haven't had a cigarette in eight years," he said. "It took me three years to quit. I smoked since I was 18, my first year in the minor leagues. I was determined to quit. My habit was at the ballpark, so when I retired I decided to quit. The last hurdle was to be around a smoker in a bar or restaurant and not have the urge to smoke."

Hernandez sometimes wonders what his career and life would have been like had he stayed in St. Louis, but those thoughts disappear pretty quickly. In many ways he still considers himself a Cardinal. He still has a Cardinals jersey in one of the upstairs bedrooms in his Florida townhouse.

"I grew up a Cardinal; I was taught the Cardinal way to play," Hernandez said. "It was so ingrained in you the pride it was to be a Cardinal. The Cardinals are the National League's version of the Yankees."

When he was playing for the Cardinals, Hernandez enjoyed a great deal of success. He won a batting title. He was the co-MVP of the National League in 1979 with the Pirates' Willie Stargell. And he earned his first World Series ring.

The seventh game of the 1982 Series is often replayed on ESPN Classic. If Hernandez happens to stumble across the video while he is changing channels he will stop and watch, but he doesn't have to see the video to remember what he was feeling that chilly October night.

"I was so nervous," he said. "I remember I went 0 for 15 in the first four games of the Series and I wound up going 7 for 11 the last three games with 8 RBIs. I remember the ninth inning of Game 7, as Bruce [Sutter] was on to save it. That usually means the other team can forget it.

"I had a pit, a knot, in my stomach. It was like an ulcer. I couldn't even bend over to get in my fielding position. I've never had that in my life. I was out there at first base thinking, 'Don't hit the ball to me.'"

Luckily for Hernandez, Sutter struck out Gorman Thomas for the final out, and the Cardinals could celebrate.

When he was playing for the Mets, Hernandez got to enjoy the thrill of winning another World Series. And he also got the thrill of playing in numerous classic games against the Cardinals. He ticks them off as if they were played yesterday—Strawberry's game-winning homer off the clock; Terry Pendleton's clutch hit in New York; all of the games down the stretch in the tight pennant race in 1987.

He was glad that he was able to help mold the Mets into a team, as he had done in St. Louis, where baseball was the primary topic on everybody's mind. That's another aspect he thinks is often lacking in today's game.

Thanks to baseball, Hernandez has been able to fulfill most of his goals in life. He has no incomplete burning desire. He would like to go on a safari in Africa; he would like to take a sailboat to Hawaii. He wants to start scuba diving again.

"I don't see anything major ahead for me," Hernandez said. "I did what I wanted to do. I don't have any great driving passion in my life."

Like everyone who lives in New York, his life and his priorities changed on September 11, 2001. His apartment faces south, but his view of the twin towers was blocked by a bank building.

"Everybody in New York lost somebody they knew," Hernandez said. "It affected everybody. I hadn't been to church in a long time, and I occasionally go to church now. It was a tragic thing. The world has changed."

6 Tom Herr

For the better part of a week, scraps of paper, scissors, and tape have covered Tom and Kim Herr's kitchen table at their home in Lancaster, Pennsylvania. It's the freshman science project at Hempfield High School—designing a paper container that will allow an egg to drop two stories without breaking.

It was the desire to spend time with sons Aaron and Jordan that led Herr to walk away from baseball at the age of 35 in 1991, when Aaron was 10 and Jordan 5. He could have continued to play, or he could have moved into managing or coaching in the minors, but those goals were not as important to him then as watching his sons grow up.

Eleven years later, as he spends most of a Sunday afternoon working with Jordan on that science project, Herr is convinced more than ever that he made the right choice.

"I figured maybe that was a good time for me to step aside," Herr said as he relaxed on the couch in the basement of the home he and Kim had built in their hometown in 1985. "I wasn't sure if it was the right decision. It was getting more and more difficult to get them in school and out of school. All of the uprooting that a baseball life can create in a family was getting harder and harder."

Herr had seen more than his share of families split apart because of baseball. As much as he loved the game, it was easy to admit that he loved his family more. He and Kim were married in 1978 and will celebrate their 25th wedding anniversary—a rare milestone for a baseball player—in 2003. The couple's home is within miles of where both grew up, and both sets of grandparents have been very active in Aaron's and Jordan's lives.

Through the years, Herr has found a way to combine his love of his family with his love of sports—volunteering as an assistant coach at Aaron and Jordan's high school for the football, basketball, and baseball teams—all three sports in which he starred when he was a student at Hempfield in the seventies.

"Coaching is a two- or threefold thing for me," Herr said. "I get to spend time with my kids; it allows me to still be around the athletic arena and involved in competition. That's therapeutic for an ex-athlete. The juices that used to flow as an athlete still flow as a coach because you are still directly involved with the outcome of the competition."

He has played a role in developing Aaron and Jordan's athletic ability, but he won't take much credit for it. Anyone who saw Aaron constantly wearing his baseball uniform and tagging along after his dad in the early eighties at Busch Stadium and other major league ballparks isn't surprised that he turned out to be a player himself—getting drafted by the Atlanta Braves as a sandwich pick between the first and second rounds in 2000. A shortstop, Aaron was expected to spend the 2002 season playing for the Braves' Class A farm team in Macon, Georgia.

"He grew up around the game," Herr said. "He grew up playing catch with Ozzie Smith, Kirby Puckett, and Mike Schmidt. That was just a part of his whole growing-up process. He was around the clubhouse all the time; he was the batboy for games in the heat of a pennant race. He grew up around that lifestyle.

"He saw how guys threw the ball, and he imitated them, and that was a big help to him. He developed the small motor skills that a baseball player needs at a very young age. What he needed to do was develop himself as an athlete to become a viable prospect, and he worked hard in the weight room to do that."

Watching Aaron develop did not bring back many flashbacks for Herr, because his athletic experiences in high school were much different. He was not drafted as a baseball player, and if he had had his first choice, he likely would have pursued basketball.

"I had my sights set on having a college basketball career," Herr said. "I was being recruited to play basketball by a few different schools, including Duke. I was planning on going to Duke, which had an interim coach. Then they brought in Bill Foster as coach, and I got a letter from him saying they had their own guys they were recruiting, and since they had never seen me play, it probably would be better for me to go somewhere else.

"I had pretty much blown everybody else off because I thought I was going to Duke, and it wasn't all that easy to call those schools back and say I was interested now. They had moved on to other players."

Herr made plans to attend the University of Delaware and actually thought he would attempt to play all three sports—football, basketball, and baseball—to see which worked out the best. Before he left for school, however, after a summer of playing American Legion ball, he finally got noticed by scouts from several teams and decided to sign with the Cardinals.

He did go to Delaware for a couple of years, getting about halfway toward a degree, while playing in the minor leagues before his baseball career took off to the point where he decided not to go back to school.

With Aaron, baseball scouts began noticing him early, and Herr was convinced Aaron was good enough that he would get drafted.

"We had such a great exciting time to see him develop as a player, to see the scouts come and watch him play," Herr said. "We had the whole excitement of the draft, and draft day, listening to it on the Internet. Those were all things I had never experienced.

"I can honestly say it's much harder on me now being a parent than it was being a player. As a player you just roll with the punches and survive. As a parent you don't feel like you have any control over things. I sit here during the summer, waiting to get a phone call from him to see how he did that night. It's almost excruciating to go through that. I want him to do well, and at this stage he's got so much to learn and has to go through the bad times to get to the good times. He's still at the crawling stage.

"It will be fun to see him progress. I can almost tell before he says anything by the tone of his voice if he had a good night or a bad night. Looking back on my career I never had to do that. I would call my parents maybe once a week, you just didn't call home every night back then. You couldn't follow my progress every day on the Internet. My dad would get the newspapers sent to him, but they would always be three or four days late. It's harder on Aaron, but he also is starting his career at a much more advantageous position than I did."

What Herr was able to give Aaron, and Jordan, and the other kids he coaches at the high school, is the knowledge and advice of someone who did play the game and knows what it takes to be successful. As time has gone by, however, he is known more now around town as Aaron and Jordan's dad than as Tom Herr, former major leaguer.

While Aaron was able to see and appreciate his father's succeeding at the major league level, Jordan was too young to remember those days. He also is different physically than Aaron, standing 6'1" as a freshman.

"I am really looking forward to Jordan's high school career because he has some things you can't teach," Herr said. "He's got a good body, he's got a good work ethic, and what I have is an understanding of how to get him prepared so when people look at him they will see what you want them to see. There is a lot of responsibility on both Aaron and Jordan because of me, but they also know they have to do it themselves.

"I can tell any kid, 'Here is what you need to do,' but if they don't want to do that, my telling them isn't going to make any difference. Sometimes those intangibles are the differences that prevent a kid from reaching his potential. I had an almost obsessive-compulsive personality. I would go out in the driveway and shoot baskets for hours, almost every night. It didn't matter if it was raining, and if it was snowing, I would shovel the driveway and I'd be out there shooting. That was just something I loved to do and wanted to do, so I put the time in.

"You can't make a kid do that. I'm not going to take him out to the driveway and make him shoot for two hours because that's what I did. But I know that if he doesn't do that, he's not going to be a real good player. That's a choice he's going to have to make."

Herr knows about choices, and many of the ones he has made have put his family before his career. Just last year, he turned down an offer to become a minor league manager, believing it would not be fair to not spend Jordan's high school years with him as he had with Aaron.

He has not abandoned his dream of becoming a manager, especially in the major leagues, which was what most baseball experts expected him to do when he was finished playing. He hopes he gets another chance in a few years, because he knows he can do the job.

"Baseball is what I know the best, and I understand the professional game and like the day-to-day aspect of it," Herr said. "From the time I was 18 until I stopped playing, it was basically the only life I knew. I have a lot of knowledge about the game, which I think would be valuable to young players. That is something that can be passed on."

Even when he was a young player, Herr was more analytical about the game than a lot of his peers. He understands the nuances of the game and the reasons behind a manager's moves. He was the type of player reporters flocked to after games, even if he was not the player of the game, because they knew he would offer an accurate and balanced account of what happened.

"In my mind I think if he had stayed in baseball and gone to the minor leagues he eventually would have managed in the majors," said

Whitey Herzog. "He was a sharp baseball guy. He would never screw up fundamentally. In watching Tommy play for as long as I did, I have to say he was one hell of a player. He was probably as good a crunch-time player as any player I've ever managed. In the last two months of every season, Tom Herr was a ballplayer."

Herr came up to the Cardinals briefly in 1979 and 1980, and it was shortly after Herzog took over as manager that he knew he had something special in Herr—ironically, when he called him into the manager's office to tell him he was sending him back down to Triple A.

"I told him, 'I'm going to send you out because I want you playing every day,'" Herzog said. "He said, 'I don't want to be sitting here. I want to play.' I told him the next time you get back here you will be here to stay. Right then and there I knew he had enough confidence in his ability that he could play."

Herr was attracting interest from other teams, and when Herzog began discussions with the Chicago Cubs about acquiring Bruce Sutter, the two players the Cubs wanted in return were Leon Durham and Herr. Herzog could move Durham because he had Keith Hernandez at first base, but he didn't want to trade Herr. He wanted to play Herr at second and move Ken Oberkfell to third. He eventually talked the Cubs into trading Sutter for Durham and Ken Reitz.

Herr was glad he got to stay in St. Louis and become a teammate of Sutter's. Herr's older brother Jeff had been a teammate of Sutter's in Legion ball in Lancaster, which is also Sutter's hometown. When Herr was in the eighth grade, he remembered, Sutter was a dominating, overpowering high school pitcher.

With Sutter becoming the most dominating closer of his era and a defensive infield that Herzog believes was second to none in baseball history, the Cardinals won the 1982 World Series. Herr's only regret was that at age 26, in only his second full major league season, he didn't really appreciate the victory as much as he later wished he had.

"I was too stupid to really understand what was going on," he said. "Being young and experiencing a world championship was great, but it was something you almost took for granted: 'Oh, this will happen a lot.' Once you go through your career and look back on it, then you realize how special it is. I appreciate the game more now, the tradition of the game more, the great players who played the game before me, with me, and after me. I have more respect for the game."

That respect is evident in the pictures and other memorabilia hanging on the walls in Herr's basement. His favorites are five framed photographs of the five stadiums he played in as his home park in the majors—with the Cardinals, the Twins, the Phillies, the Mets, and the Giants. In another room in the basement are the framed jerseys he wore for those five teams. Also hanging in his basement is a painting that was done from a photo of Herr and Aaron sitting together in the dugout.

During most of his career, Herr thought he was going to play for only one team—the Cardinals. He was caught totally off guard on that April day in 1988 when Herzog called him into his office, and he and General Manager Dal Maxvill told Herr he had been traded to the Twins for Tom Brunansky.

"The shock of the trade bothered me more than anything," he said. "There had been no rumors, no inkling of any kind, no hints of anything happening. I was a Cardinal. We had just been to the World Series again. I was one of the main guys. I wanted to play my whole career there. It really hit me out of the blue.

"I can remember getting on the plane to fly to Minneapolis and crying like a baby. It was hard to go through. Looking back on it, I didn't handle it very well. I kept looking back instead of looking forward. I was looking at it more that the Cardinals didn't want me than that the Twins wanted me. If I had put a more positive spin on it, I would have reacted better. I had to do some serious regrouping on the plane, because I was a basket case."

Herr was eligible for free agency at the end of the season, and he told the Twins he was not interested in re-signing with them. They traded him to the Phillies, close to Herr's home, and he rebounded to accept his post-Cardinals life. Then came another unexpected trade, to the Mets, and finally a move to the Giants, and then Herr decided it was time to go. He didn't want to be a vagabond player, moving from team to team every year.

He also was able to erase the bad memories of his departure from St. Louis and remember the good times—the three pennants in six seasons—instead.

Those were happy days, but so is the present. During his career, Herr was able to structure his contracts so that he could defer money until after he was 40 years old, so he would have time to be home and not have to worry about earning a living. He has been involved in one business venture—a store selling baseball equipment and specialty items—but it never was a success, and Herr closed it after about three years.

His self-published book, *A View from Second Base,* was designed as a guide to baseball strategy and instruction for coaches, players, and fans. The book did well enough to go into a second printing.

He also has remained active in his church and other Christian activities, teaching an adult Sunday school class and going with a group to Ecuador in 1989 to help a small village build a church.

"We at least got the foundation and construction started," Herr said. "It was a great experience because it gave me an awareness of what people who are not as fortunate as we are have to go through. There are so many things that we just take for granted."

All of his blessings, for his family and his baseball career, aren't something Herr takes for granted. He believes he worked hard at both, and he has no regrets about any of the choices he made along the way.

He is glad he has had the opportunity to pass along the knowledge he gained about baseball to his own sons, as well as to other young players.

"Baseball is a game of failure," Herr said. "A good hitter is still going to make an out 7 out of every 10 at-bats. You have to teach kids to accept that as part of the game, to understand it and not get frustrated by it. By the same token, you have to not get frustrated as a parent and make them press a little bit. If you can get anything across to them it's to keep turning the page, going forward, trying to take something positive away from each at-bat and try to build on it. Kids are so results-oriented that it's tough because they can't see anything good out of making an out."

Herr won't be surprised if one day in the future he is watching Aaron playing in the major leagues. He thinks Jordan has an athletic career ahead of him as well, if that is what he chooses to do.

When he was playing, Herr tried not to look too far into the future, and he's trying to keep that philosophy now regarding his sons' careers. He is glad to live in the present, occupying his time with projects like designing the perfect container to let an egg drop two stories and not break.

"It didn't quite land properly, because the egg rolled out of the top," reported Herr. "It didn't break though, and the whole goal was not to break the egg. I hope he gets an A."

7 | Dane Iorg

Good wood to Dane Iorg used to mean a great baseball bat. It is still important for him to find good wood today, but for an entirely different reason.

Iorg is working these days as the sales manager for Capital Lumber Co. in Salt Lake City, a company that sells wholesale lumber to retail outlets in Utah and Idaho. As someone who grew up in the lumber mills in northern California, Iorg considers this a perfect job for him.

Maybe it's not quite as perfect as playing baseball, but Iorg knew that wouldn't last forever. He retired after spending the 1986 season with the Padres and moved back to his home in Utah.

"I tried a couple of other sales things, but then a friend of mine called me and asked if I wanted to get involved with this," Iorg said. "I've been here ever since."

Unlike his brother Garth, who also played in the major leagues, Iorg decided while he was playing that he would most likely not stay in baseball once his career was over. A devoted family man, he thought that it wouldn't be fair to his wife and kids to still be away from home so much and not be playing.

Garth spent years managing in the minor leagues and was the first-base coach for the Toronto Blue Jays until June 2002.

"I've got eight kids," Iorg said, "ranging in age from 28 to 9—five boys and three girls. Only three are left at home now though, so the house seems kind of quiet."

While Iorg enjoyed some quality years with the Cardinals, including hitting .529 with four doubles in helping the Cardinals win the 1982 World Series, he is best remembered by St. Louis fans in a negative way. It was Iorg, playing for Kansas City, who got the base hit to win the sixth game of the 1985 World Series for the Royals—moments after Don Denkinger's missed call at first base prevented the Cardinals from closing out the Series.

Iorg admits it was a strange moment.

"I had better friends on the Cardinals than on the Royals," Iorg said. "Todd Worrell [who gave up the hit] was a really good friend. When you get on the field, however, you have to put all the friendships out the window. The only thing Todd said to me was that if anybody was going to get the hit, he was glad it was me."

The hit became magnified even more the next day when the Royals pounded the Cardinals 11-0 to complete the Series victory.

"I really enjoyed all of my years in St. Louis," Iorg said. "[Darrell] Porter was probably my closest friend on the team. I had a lot of respect for Ozzie [Smith] on and off the field. What really made the 1982 season special was my teammates. Everybody had a great level of commitment and played hard every day."

One of the reasons Iorg enjoyed those days so much is he really understood and appreciated all of the hard work he had put in just to make it to the major leagues. He did not reach the major leagues to stay until he was 28 years old.

"Some of us had a little tougher path to get there, and maybe that's why it seemed a little more satisfying," Iorg said. "You got to take a breath and say you finally made it. It was a dream since I was a young boy."

It was also special because of the Cardinals fans, Iorg said. Baseball players who never get a chance to experience what it is like to be a Cardinal are really missing out, he said.

"St. Louis is a special baseball place," Iorg said. "The fans are so supportive. Unless a player has come from another place, I don't think he realizes how special St. Louis is."

It also took a little while after he had retired for Iorg to further appreciate how special it was, and how lucky he was, to have played major league baseball. He wouldn't trade those memories for anything, but he is happy now that he has found a life after baseball that is just as fulfilling.

"It took me a little while to find out what I was good at," he said. "I love what I am doing."

8 | Tito Landrum

As he slides into a seat in the lounge off the lobby of the Grand Hyatt hotel in midtown Manhattan, there is a quick indication of what life after baseball has been like for Tito Landrum. He now goes by his given first name, Terry.

"My mother gave it to me, and I'm proud of it, and so is she," Landrum says. "When I sent her some stories home when I was in the minor leagues, she said, 'Who is Tito? Is he related to us?' Once baseball was over I went back to Terry."

Landrum had become Tito in 1973, when he was playing for the Cardinals' Class A minor league team in Orangeburg, South Carolina. He was rooming with three Latin players, and they had a hard time pronouncing Terry. The Jackson Five was popular at the time, including Tito Jackson, and the three told Landrum one day that they were going to start calling him Tito. The name stuck.

It followed him throughout his years in the minors and his nine years in the major leagues—through two stints with the Cardinals, two stints with the Orioles, and his year in Los Angeles with the Dodgers. Those years produced many happy memories, but when baseball ended, Landrum was ready to quit—he just wasn't certain what he was ready to do next.

The woman he had met and fallen in love with, Carol Williams, took a job as an executive producer with ABC's *World News Tonight* with Peter Jennings in New York, so the couple packed up in March 1992 and moved from St. Louis to New York, something both had sworn they would never do. A decade later, they are still there.

"Every time I played here I said there was no way I would live here," Landrum said. "Carol said the same thing. It was written into her contract that if we hated New York after a year we could move to Washington, D.C., or Atlanta. Here we are. It grew on us."

During his first few months in New York, Williams was working and Landrum was unsure what he wanted to do. Through friends in the media, he tried some broadcasting and announcing and speech classes but came away unfulfilled. People for years had thought he would become a model, but he was told he was too short. Finally one day Williams asked him what he really wanted to do. The answer was that he wanted to become a physical therapist.

Because of what he had gone through in recovering from injuries himself, including back surgery, Landrum had some idea of what a physical therapist did. He had designed his own rehabilitation pro- gram, and he thought his experiences as an athlete would blend well with the medical knowledge of how to recover from injuries.

The challenge that goal presented, however, was returning to school. Landrum was 39 years old, and he had completed one quar- ter of one year in junior college, and that was more than 20 years earlier. He agreed to take a biology class at New York University and see what happened.

"The only time I have ever seen him afraid was going to that first class," Carol said. "He was afraid he was going to fail."

However Landrum, a C-plus student in high school, knew he was more focused on this goal than he had been as an 18-year-old stu- dent. He knew that to reach his goal of earning a degree in physi- cal therapy, he had to do well in his early classes. Only students with a B-plus average were admitted to the program, and only a small percentage of students who were qualified actually were accepted. Landrum made the grades and was accepted on his first try. Other students had been passed over two, three, or four times.

For the next five years, Landrum was dedicated and focused on earning his college degree. A study group met at his apartment every weekend, sometimes spending the night on the floor. One summer, Landrum was working on Long Island from 9:00 A.M. until 2:00 or 2:30 P.M., then had to be back in Manhattan for a class at 4:00 P.M. "It was a terrible summer; it was the toughest eight weeks of my life." But he got the grades he needed, and that gave him the confidence that he could pass and complete the program.

The degree came in 1998 and produced one of the best moments of Landrum's life, in or out of baseball. Even though there were students in the School of Education with higher grade point averages, Landrum's fellow classmates named him as the valedictorian. He was voted the honor of delivering a speech at the graduation ceremonies at Carnegie Hall. His speech was short but inspirational.

"Today I am a 43-year-old college graduate," Landrum said during his speech. "When I started college in my late thirties, I was more frightened than I'd been in my entire life. I was surrounded by teenagers, really smart teenagers. Teenagers who'd been studying hard while I was watching my former career evaporate. When you stop being a professional baseball player, you suddenly remember that no one told you what to do next. And I had no idea what to do.

"Somehow I pushed down the fear and tried one class. It felt a lot like my first day in A ball, except when I was in the minors I was the same age as my teammates. But I got through it. And I kept going. And when I did poorly on a test or poorly in class, I remembered it took me eight years to get to the major leagues. The average player takes four.

"A minister I admire told me a story once that I used to lift my spirits when I was playing baseball. As the story goes, three men were running a race. The fastest man kept looking over his shoulder to see how the others were doing. The second fastest was preoccupied with himself looking at his shoes to see if his laces were untied. Both tripped and fell. But the slowest kept his gaze fixed on the finish line and won the race.

"I've always identified with the slowest runner. I spent eight long years in the minors, then I made it to three World Series. Not one of them felt as good as it feels to be here today."

Landrum settled into his life as a physical therapist, treating as many as 19 clients a day. He received referrals from doctors and surgeons and began working with many athletes, including college baseball players and others coming off surgery for torn anterior cruciate ligaments or a torn rotator cuff. Because he had been an athlete and had overcome his own serious injuries, Landrum was well qualified for his new job.

Williams had changed jobs over the years, moving to NBC as an executive producer in charge of producing various shows for high-end cable outlets. They had adapted well enough to New York, taking advantage of what the city has to offer and learning to tolerate or forget the rest, when the lives of everyone in the city changed in a few minutes on the morning of September 11, 2001.

Landrum was working for Plus One, and the company had two offices in lower Manhattan. One was in the American Express building, the other across the street. Both buildings were within a block of the World Trade Center towers.

"By the grace of God, I had a doctor's appointment that morning or I would have been in the office in the American Express building," Landrum said. "I came out of the doctor's office and saw all the ruckus."

Landrum was able to get through to Williams to make certain she was all right, but then all of the phones in midtown Manhattan went out. He could not call his mother, and only when a high school friend somehow got through on his cell phone the next day was Landrum able to tell his friend to call his mother and tell her he was all right.

All of the employees in his company's offices escaped unharmed. Two people were missing for a while, but then company officials learned they were safe. While Landrum knows he would have survived the initial attack, he never will know what he would have done had he been in the office that fateful morning.

"I don't know how much I would have been able to run in and help people, but I'm sure there would have been some thought to it," he said. "Everybody down there was thinking about trying to help other people. It was just a horrifying experience."

Neither Landrum nor Williams lost any relatives or close friends in the attack, but they were lucky. One of Landrum's clients was a neighbor and close friend of a flight attendant who was on one of the planes. At the street level of their apartment building is a fire station, and 11 firefighters from that station were killed.

"It was so hard, and it's still hard," Landrum said. "Honestly I didn't leave the house for a month. I couldn't move. It has definitely changed me, even though I can't really put a finger on how. I wanted to go down to the site to help out, but all you could really do was pass out water and clap and cheer for the people who were working at the rescue. The smell was terrible, and the sight was more terrifying.

"I actually appreciate life a lot more, the experiences I have with people. You know how you go by somebody and say, 'Hi, how are you, how are you doing?' I listen more now, and I'm more attentive to things of that nature. I have a greater appreciation and understanding that we are here for a short period of time. I'm not walking around corners blindly anymore. It matured me.

"It was like we were in a third-world country or Beirut with the concrete barriers on the street, and we could stand and look out our windows and see all of the smoke. I respect the people of New York for all they have gone through, and I think they have weathered it very well. I have a newfound respect for them. I am proud to live here."

The attack forced Landrum to change jobs. All of the paperwork at his company was lost, and with both offices destroyed, the company had to relocate to another small office and took only the workers with the most seniority. Luckily, he did find another job, and business has been booming.

In fact, Landrum is so busy these days that he is trying to cut down on the number of clients he sees each day, especially during the spring, when he has an additional job working as an assistant coach with the NYU baseball team.

When Landrum was in school at NYU, one of the athletic administrators saw his two World Series rings and made the connection that he was the Landrum who had played baseball, even though that was Tito and his name now was Terry. He asked Landrum to help out the head coach, and Landrum has been doing it now for six years.

Baseball at NYU is a club sport, not a varsity sport, and it has presented Landrum with some interesting challenges. When flyers were passed out telling students interested in the baseball club to come to a meeting, one student showed up thinking it was going to be a club of students who wanted to trade baseball cards. Another player is a former sergeant in the Israeli Army who had never played before. Landrum had to teach him how to stand and hold the bat and had to tell him the game was divided into innings, not sets.

"It's wonderful to see these kids playing for fun, the way we used to," Landrum said. "And we've got kids who are dedicated."

Because it is a club sport, the team has to fight for a time and place to practice. The school does not have a home field, and the team cannot get the use of the gym except from 10:00 P.M. until midnight or 1:00 A.M. on Mondays. The team has hitting practice on Wednesday nights from 8:00 P.M. until 10:00 P.M. and then practices Fridays on Staten Island.

Little wonder that when Landrum goes home at night or on the weekends, all he wants to do is relax.

Home is an apartment on the 39th floor of a Manhattan high-rise, overlooking Lincoln Center and the Hudson River. Landrum and Williams are happy there, even though they can open their floor-to-ceiling windows a total of only five inches. They are called stockbroker windows, Williams says, without having to offer an explanation.

"My dad was in the air force, and that was a transient lifestyle," said Landrum, who lived in 10 states and three countries before he graduated from high school. "We moved every two years. Baseball was a transient lifestyle, moving all the time. When I retired, I wanted a place to put my feet up and call home. It's quiet and peaceful, and it's our sanctuary. You can just sit there and stare out the windows. We face south, and on a clear day you can see the Statue of Liberty.

"This city is a concrete jungle, and you can't get out and smell the grass unless you go to Central Park, and then it's mostly dog poop that you smell. I'm still looking for grass under my feet and a backyard, and we'll get it someday."

Neither Landrum nor Williams owns a car, because it would cost them $400 a month to park it and another $2,400 a year to insure it. They just rent a car on the odd occasions when they need to drive someplace. They go to the ballet and the museums and sporting events, and usually Landrum is anonymous, which he says might be the best thing of all about New York.

"One of the scariest things that has happened to me in New York was when I was in school," Landrum said. "We had a party one night down in Hell's Kitchen, and it was about 2:00 in the morning. I walked a friend home, and then I started walking home. It was about 20 blocks or so. I passed by this man, and he looked at me and said, 'Tito, how you doing?' It scared the hell out of me. All I could do was say fine and keep walking. I turned around to watch him, and he just kept walking and never turned around to see me. I have no idea who he was or how he knew who I was.

"Another time I was standing on the sidewalk, and this man with an accent came up to me and said, 'Red white blue.' I asked him what he meant, and he said, 'You wore uniform, red white blue, Cardinals, 21.' That was my number. Somehow he recognized me too."

One time while he was playing, Landrum was mistaken for somebody else. He was standing in the lobby of the Grand Hyatt, where the Cardinals stayed when they were in New York, and he was wearing a suit. "Mrs. Busch, the wife of the Cardinals' owner, was on the trip, and she noticed me and said, 'Young man, can you go get my bags?' I said, 'I would love to, but I don't work here.' She had no idea who I was. Then she said again, 'Just get them for me.' I told her again that I didn't work there.

59

"When we got to the stadium, the game was about to start and she was sitting in the box seats right by the dugout. I walked up to her and said, 'Did you ever get your bags, ma'am?' I still don't think she ever knew who I was."

Most baseball fans, especially in St. Louis, do remember Landrum. He played 79 games for the Cardinals in 1982 but was not placed on the postseason roster. Disappointed, he still traveled with the team to Atlanta and Milwaukee and enjoyed the experience.

He kept telling himself there would be more opportunities in the future, and he didn't have to wait long. Traded to Baltimore the next year, he found himself in the playoffs against the White Sox. Batting in the tenth inning of Game 4, his home run off Britt Burns snapped a scoreless tie and ignited a three-run rally that gave the Orioles the American League pennant. The Orioles then defeated the Phillies to win the World Series.

Two years later, Landrum was back in St. Louis and was platooning regularly in the outfield. The Cardinals won the division title, and when Vince Coleman was knocked out of the postseason after he was run over by an automatic tarpaulin machine, Landrum found himself in the starting lineup.

He hit .429 in helping the Cardinals beat the Dodgers and was one of the few Cardinals who hit well—a .360 average—in the World Series loss to Kansas City.

Whitey Herzog certainly appreciated what Landrum brought to the Cardinals.

"He never probably dreamed he would make the big leagues," Herzog said. "He played like hell for us. He was a good bench player because he kept his mouth shut and he knew his role. He was just happy to be there."

Those were happy memories, but Landrum still says his best moment was in 1980—his first career at-bat in the major leagues, when he came up to bat against the Dodgers' Terry Forster and grounded out to Steve Garvey.

"I got a standing ovation," he said. "That's how nice the people in St. Louis are."

Of all the special people he has met through baseball, there is no doubt who is first on his list. Landrum, who has two daughters from a previous marriage, one of whom lives in St. Louis while the other is a student at Florida State University, met Williams when she was working for a St. Louis station. He said the players gave her the nickname "Legs." The two have been together since 1986.

"Carol has been the best thing in my life," he said. "I knew what I was doing in baseball to the point where I would put aside family and friends to get to where I wanted in baseball. At the end of my career she was very inspirational. She has a tremendous mind. I carried a dictionary with me so I could understand her. She would say a word, then I would have to try to remember it and figure out how to spell it so I could look it up and see what it meant.

"There are times when Carol gets very upset at people who don't try. When it came to getting an education, I didn't try because I was afraid I would fail. She sat down with me many times to help me out, not just with school but life in general. Because of baseball everything had just been handed to us. Players really are prima donnas. I didn't know a whole hell of a lot about life, and it has made a tremendous difference for her to be around me. She gave me the kind of support I needed to be where I am today."

Where Landrum is today is New York, and he is certain he still will be there for the near future. In the not-too-distant future, however, he and Williams plan to get out of the city and head west, probably landing in Colorado.

"Carol is from Colorado, and I am from Albuquerque, so somewhere in between would be nice," he said. "My mother got sick, and I went home for a month and a half, and I really enjoyed it. I enjoyed getting in the car and going to the grocery store. Here you just pick up the phone and everything is delivered to you—groceries, laundry, everything. You can order anything from anywhere at anytime. Do I want to get out of here? You better believe it. I would love it."

As was the case throughout his baseball career, and with his life since, Landrum has no worry about what the future holds.

"I really was in the right place at the right time for just about everything," he said.

9 | Dave LaPoint

The scene is repeated over and over. At George's restaurant, on the shores of Lake George. At O'Toole's, where his framed jersey number 39 from the 1982 World Series hangs. Even when he goes to Poopie's for lunch, the greeting is the same.

Dave LaPoint, it seems, can't go anywhere in his hometown of Glens Falls, New York, and not run into somebody he knows or be greeted by a friendly, "Hi, Dave" as he comes in the door.

"It is a small town," LaPoint points out.

Even though LaPoint left the town of 16,000 to begin playing professional baseball when he was 18 years old, now 25 years ago, he never really left. He returned every off-season of his career except one, and when his career ended in 1991, he didn't think of going anyplace but home.

He is one of four former major leaguers to hail from Glens Falls, New York, joining Johnny Podres, Dave Palmer, and Randy St. Claire. Only he and St. Claire still live in the area, and that makes them the local celebrities.

"But the most famous guy from town is probably Hacksaw Duggan, who retired a couple of years ago from the pro wrestling tour," LaPoint said. "Wrestling is really big up here, but he lives in Florida."

LaPoint has been involved in several activities since returning to Glens Falls full time. He opened and still owns a bar in the middle of town, called Pitchers. He spent two years working as the general manager and manager of a team in the independent Northeast League, the Adirondack Lumberjacks. He also is a frequent visitor to the schools his three children attend. People recognize him in the grocery store, at the bank, wherever he happens to stop.

"This is a pretty humbling area," LaPoint said. "Usually back here if you get out of line people put you in your place. I've never considered that I've been any different or acted any different. I'm just a guy from Glens Falls, New York, who mixed in and got along with everybody. That's in your eyes.

"You could walk down the street and not say hi to somebody because you didn't hear them and all of a sudden you're a prima donna, you're too good, you can't say something to somebody. It's part of the job."

If he had so chosen, LaPoint certainly had the credentials to return to town and act as if he was somebody important after his career, which lasted more than 13 seasons and saw him pitch almost 10 years in the majors. He started 21 games in the Cardinals' championship season of 1982, plus Game 4 in the World Series. He pitched for his home-state team, the Yankees, and was an Opening Day starter three times.

Of all of his years in the majors and all of the teams he played for, none stands out like the 1982 Cardinals. It was special partially because he was 23 years old and partially because he made the Opening Day roster for the first time in his career. But he said the main reason it was special was because of all of the people he was able to associate with on a daily basis.

"We left St. Petersburg to open the season in Houston, and one of the newspaper writers, Jack Herman, got up to use the restroom just after we left," LaPoint said. "Some of the players got a crazy idea, so they threw all of the equipment bags in front of the door so he couldn't get out. He was ringing the bell, but they had already paid off the flight attendants not to go back there. He had to ride in the bathroom all the way from St. Pete to Houston.

"Then on Opening Day, we went out and beat Nolan Ryan and the Astros 14–3. I said if Nolan Ryan gets beat 14–3, I don't stand a chance in this game. I'm not even going to unpack."

With a manager such as Whitey Herzog and veteran players including Bruce Sutter, Jim Kaat, Gene Tenace, and Keith Hernandez on the roster, LaPoint didn't know what kind of season he was headed for, but he quickly found out.

"The very first week, I was trying to leave after a game and I was just going out of the clubhouse to go home when Tenace grabbed me by the collar and said, 'Sit down, kid.'" LaPoint said. "He said, 'You're pitching this week, right? Sit here and listen. We're going to talk about the game and see if you learned anything tonight.' We did that over and over. That's how I learned to pitch. That's how I learned to play the game.

"I remember pitching a game against Pittsburgh. I had two outs in the first inning and nobody on and I struck out Bill Madlock on a change-up. I came in after the inning and Hernandez put me up against the wall. He said, 'What are you doing?' I said, 'I don't know, I just struck out Bill Madlock.' He said, 'What happens when he comes up in the seventh inning with men on base and you've got to get him out. What are you going to throw then? Are you going to tell me you couldn't have gotten him out there with something else? Now you've just wasted your best pitch in a non-RBI situation.' I said, 'Man, I'm sorry. I didn't know.' But after that I did. Those were the little things they did that made the team successful."

At the start of the season, the starting rotation was in doubt behind Joaquin Andujar and Bob Forsch. It was in May that Herzog moved both rookies, LaPoint and John Stuper, into the rotation.

"They pitched great," Herzog said. "They really did a job. LaPoint lived on his change-up, one of the greatest I've ever seen. Guys would know he was going to throw it, and they still couldn't hit it. He was a character. He would do imitations of all of the public-address announcers and would have everybody on the bus rolling in the aisle because they were laughing so hard."

Thinking back to those happy times makes LaPoint smile, as do other memories such as Kaat, older then than LaPoint is now, asking if LaPoint could come to the ballpark early the next day so he could teach Kaat his slidestep change-up. He remembers nobody ever second-guessing a decision by Herzog, even if it didn't work out how he had planned. He remembers pitching coach Hub Kittle standing in a hotel lobby at 3:00 in the morning, trying to teach a bellman how to throw a forkball.

Flying from St. Louis to Cincinnati once, Kaat and Sutter told rookie pitcher Jeff Lahti that instead of turning his watch ahead one hour, because it was such a short flight, he should turn his watch up 45 minutes. "He missed the bus by 15 minutes four days in a row," LaPoint said.

LaPoint also remembers winning 35 games in a Cardinals uniform during his career, and Sutter earning the save in 33 of them.

"If you got the hitter to hit a ground ball, he was out," LaPoint said. "If you had a lead after the seventh inning, you won. How great was that? Those were the things that made it easier."

It also made it easier to have a manager like Herzog, although LaPoint admits he was getting a little worried toward the end of the season when he had not pitched for several days in a row. He thought Herzog might be about to send him back to the minors and that he would miss out on the playoffs and the World Series.

"We were in New York, and I went out to the ballpark early and was sitting in the clubhouse playing cards by myself," LaPoint said. "I felt this hand on my shoulder, and as I looked up, Whitey was sitting down next to me. Already I was going crazy—not here, not now. He said, 'You're getting tired. You're tired physically, and you're tired mentally. I just wanted to give you a break. Now we're playing the Mets and Pirates, and you pitch good against both of those teams. I want to relieve you against them, and you will probably help us win a couple of games. Then you're going to start against

Image by Lew Portnoy, Spectra-Action Inc.

Mike Ramsey filled in for Ozzie Smith during a key stretch in the 1982 pennant race and played flawless defense.

There was nobody better than Lonnie Smith at breaking up a double play.

Image by Lew Portnoy, Spectra-Action Inc.

Image courtesy of the Baseball Hall of Fame, Cooperstown, N.Y.

Steve Mura is usually the forgotten man of the 1982 Cardinals' starting rotation, but he contributed 12 victories during the regular season.

Whether he was hitting, playing defense, or running the bases, Willie McGee always seemed to make things happen.

Image by Lew Portnoy, Spectra-Action Inc.

The 1982 World Series was Willie McGee's coming out party, making him a star for years to come.

Image by Lew Portnoy, Spectra-Action Inc.

Image courtesy of the Baseball Hall of Fame, Cooperstown, N.Y.

One of two rookies in the Cardinals' starting rotation for much of 1982, Dave LaPoint was a key contributor to the team's success.

Montreal and it will probably be the game we clinch the pennant.' Just like that.

"I relieved a couple of times, we won the games, and I started against Montreal the game we clinched the pennant. That's a man who knows his personnel and his schedule."

LaPoint didn't pitch in the sweep of the Braves that clinched the NL pennant and put the Cardinals into the World Series, but he was scheduled to start Game 4 of the Series in Milwaukee.

As the Cardinals prepared for that Series, Herzog came up to LaPoint and asked if he would like to go to Florida to pitch in the instructional league, so he could stay sharp before his start against the Brewers.

"I said, 'With all due respect, Whitey, the plane might crash,'" LaPoint said. "'Is it OK with you if I just stay here?' He said, 'If you want to stay here you stay here.'"

It was Herzog who gave LaPoint the nickname Snacks, because of his ability to eat. LaPoint said it actually was an incorrect name, because he almost never ate cakes or pies or desserts like that. If there was a hunk of cheese in the refrigerator, however, it would be hard for him to pass that up. LaPoint actually had several nicknames, including Wimpy, hung on him by Tenace.

The nickname Herzog gave him came back to haunt LaPoint during his start in Game 4. With the Cardinals leading the Series two games to one, LaPoint was pitching beautifully. Going into the bottom of the seventh, the Cardinals were leading 5–1 and were nine outs away from a commanding three-games-to-one lead in the Series.

With one out, Ben Oglivie hit a ground ball to Hernandez at first. With LaPoint covering the base, Hernandez tossed him the ball underhanded. To LaPoint's horror, he dropped the ball. The line that was repeated over and over, even years later, was that if the ball had been a hamburger, he would not have dropped it.

A broken-bat single and a bloop double followed before LaPoint got the second out. By the time three relievers were able to get the third out, the Brewers had scored six runs and went on to a 7–5 win.

"It doesn't bother me one bit," LaPoint said. "I missed it, big deal. I wish Whitey would have given me one more batter. If those two guys were going to score, let it be my fault. I was pretty confident. I was throwing good still. That had been pretty much the way I had pitched all year, however, and we had a good bullpen. Really, when you're 23 pitching in the World Series, you don't know what's right or wrong anyway."

Four days later, LaPoint found himself warming up in the bullpen before the seventh game of the Series. Andujar had been hit by a line drive in his start in Game 3, and there was concern whether he would be able to pitch. If he had been unable to pitch, LaPoint would have started the game.

"That was nerve-racking," LaPoint said. "You can't exactly ask him how he feels. 'Joaquin, how do you feel?' 'I'm one tough Dominican.' 'Well that's great, Joaquin, but how's your arm?'"

Luckily Andujar did pitch, and LaPoint sat on the bench as the Cardinals clinched the championship. When Sutter struck out Gorman Thomas for the final out, LaPoint was climbing behind his cheering teammates, trying to get as far away as possible from the guard dog he had been sitting next to in the dugout.

"The only thing I was thinking about was that I was not going to get bit by that dog," LaPoint said.

Little did LaPoint know on that night that slightly more than two years later, he would experience the worst day in his baseball career, the day he was traded by the Cardinals to the Giants for Jack Clark.

"How about the way that day started?" LaPoint said. "I was on the caravan in Illinois, and when we made our last stop, somebody asked about the latest trade rumors. Mike Shannon says, 'Let's make up a fake one, Dave LaPoint for Jack Clark.' I got off the bus, drove home, and got a phone call that I had been traded for Jack Clark.

"It was the toughest day in my baseball career. To make it worse, I was at a Blues game a couple of days later, and when I got up to leave, I got a standing ovation. I went back the next year and beat the Cardinals 5–0 and got another standing ovation. That's what you miss. That's what St. Louis is.

"After it was all done and over with, and I figured out why I had been traded so much—I was wild and I talked too much—I just wish someone along the way had taken me aside and said, 'Hey. . . .' Maybe they did and I didn't notice."

From the Giants, LaPoint moved on to the Tigers, the Padres, the Cardinals again, the White Sox, the Pirates, the Yankees, and the Phillies, following his first two career stops in Milwaukee and St. Louis, before his career ended. Somewhere along the line, his first marriage ended in divorce.

"Everything has a price, and baseball is no different," LaPoint said. "In most situations in baseball, the way I've looked at it, the same thing that attracts you to a person is the same thing that makes you unattractive later. When you meet your wife it's exciting because you're traveling, you've got money. Then you start to have kids. You want to be a father, but you're still doing what you did when you first met. I don't think most of us see the other side, what the wives and kids are going through.

"Players want to have the same schedule, do the same workouts, as they did when they were single, or at least before they had kids. That goes out the window. Part of that was being wild, and I'm not denying I was, and that's part of your personality that's taken away too. I think it all goes together. Most of us don't know when it is time to quit, or stop, and that's probably why most of us get divorced."

LaPoint, who had two children from his first marriage, later remarried and has three children with his second wife.

The one job that LaPoint thought would be a natural for him when he retired was to become a broadcaster, either doing analysis on game broadcasts or hosting a talk show. For reasons unknown, it has never happened.

"As I found out, announcers die less frequently than baseball players, so there weren't that many job openings," LaPoint said. "It's like anything else; I didn't know the right people. I thought I knew everybody, but I guess we weren't that good of friends."

The lack of an immediate broadcasting or coaching job led LaPoint in another direction. He became an agent, working for his former agents, Jim Bronner and Bob Gilhooley. It's the only job he regrets trying.

"I thought that would be an ideal job," LaPoint said. "My idea was that I was going to convince players who already had an agent but weren't happy to come sign with us. That wasn't my job. I was supposed to go out and recruit new talent. I realized that job is tougher than being an umpire. You are on the road every day, wining and dining these young players. I also wasn't any good at blowing smoke. If a guy wasn't very good, I couldn't tell him to sign with us and we would get him a zillion dollars. Jim and Bob treated me great, but I wished I hadn't tried that."

It was soon after he moved back to Glens Falls that the independent team came looking for a manager and offered the job to LaPoint, who also talked the owners into making him the general manager. Those jobs lasted two years, and even included a brief pitching comeback, before the owner sold the team and left LaPoint with several unpaid bills. He was able to negotiate a settlement with the team's new owner.

"It was a great learning experience because it was a side of baseball I had never seen before," LaPoint said. "We did everything from designing the logo to buying uniforms and screens for the field. I called Buddy Bates [the Cardinals' equipment manager] to find out how you got a pine tar rag and a resin bag. Have you ever sat there and thought where a resin bag comes from? What is a resin bag? I was promised $300,000 of working capital and ended up getting only $40,000. But we went 25–5 down the stretch and won the championship, so that made everything worthwhile."

Next came the opening of the sports bar and restaurant, Pitchers, which also turned out to be more difficult than LaPoint had expected. One aspect of the job he had not thought of in advance was the hours he would be required to work.

"These things don't close; they open every day," he said. "And here, the bars are open until 4:00 in the morning. When you open a business, you think you are going to work a couple of days and then get a day off, but it doesn't work that way. The business is notorious for people stealing stuff and losing stuff. It is about the closest thing you can do here to being in baseball, because you are a celebrity and your ego gets boosted again."

The one year he didn't send out résumés looking for a job in baseball was when Mike Jorgensen, the Cardinals' director of player development, called and offered him the job as pitching coach at Double A Arkansas. LaPoint jumped at the opportunity, hoping he could reconnect with the Cardinals for years to come.

Unfortunately for LaPoint, the relationship lasted only two years, one year at Little Rock and one year (2001) when the team moved to New Haven, Connecticut.

"Some of the parts of coaching, like the chain of command, I wasn't very good with, and that was my mistake," LaPoint said. "The bureaucracy of an organization never mattered that much to me. If I thought something was hurting one of my pitchers, I wasn't afraid to speak my mind. I don't want to ever be responsible for hurting somebody, and that's where I got in trouble."

LaPoint planned to return to an independent team in 2002, working as the pitching coach for the Long Island Ducks. He hasn't got his future life planned out too far after that, but he knows what he will most likely be doing.

"I know I can run a restaurant; I know I can do a radio show," LaPoint said. "I know I can run a baseball team."

The constant in all of those jobs is that, somehow, baseball will be part of it.

"It's in your blood," LaPoint said. "I love baseball so much I once went to dinner with Hub Kittle and Max Patkin. It was in the minor leagues some year. That was a long dinner."

10 Willie McGee

Willie McGee's promise that he will one day wear a Cardinals uniform again hasn't been forgotten. It's just on hold for a few more years while his girls grow up.

McGee pledged during Willie McGee Day in spring of 2000 that he was not finished with the Cardinals. He said he would love to coach in St. Louis—but it was time to back away from the game on a full-time basis and devote himself to the family that watched him become a superstar and one of the Cardinals' all-time greats.

The Cardinals have been honored to have Hall of Famers, All-Stars, and great players wear the "birds on the bat" jersey. During its storied history, the team has won World Series and National League pennants and is one of the game's most solid institutions.

Amazingly, a skinny kid who had never seen St. Louis until late spring of 1982 is one of the Cardinals fans' all-time favorites.

McGee is that beloved by the faithful.

His humble attitude, outstanding command of the game of baseball, and blinding speed all combined in his rail of a body when he exploded on the baseball scene. He didn't say much; he let his bat and glove do the talking.

The crescendo of an amazing 1982 season was the third game of the World Series. After splitting the first two games of the Series in St. Louis, the Cardinals and Brewers moved north to chilly, wet County Stadium in Milwaukee.

On that Friday night, McGee and the Cardinals took control of the World Series. The game was a key moment in a run of championship-level baseball that also saw the team reach the World Series in 1985 and 1987.

Manager Whitey Herzog said it might have been one of the greatest individual performances in the history of the World Series.

McGee, who hit just four home runs that rookie season, belted a pair of home runs off Milwaukee starter Pete Vuckovich. The Cardinals cruised to a 6–2 victory, but the game could have been closer if not for McGee's brilliant defense in center field. He made a running, leaping catch of a 400-foot Paul Molitor drive in the first inning that kept the Brewers off the scoreboard early.

Later in the game, he robbed Gorman Thomas of a home run in the ninth with an incredible leaping grab in which he snatched the ball from the air just as it was clearing the left-center-field wall.

On the national NBC-TV broadcasts of the first two games of the Series, there had been a humorous disagreement as to who the MVP of the game should have been.

When McGee made the catch on Thomas' drive, former broadcaster and native St. Louisan Joe Garagiola said, "If anyone votes for anyone other than Willie McGee, I'm leaving."

McGee was now a national star, although he didn't realize it yet. And even though that game provided his highlight tape for the rest of his career, he said his personal favorite moment of the Series came when Bruce Sutter struck out Thomas for the final out in Game 7.

"I had nothing to compare with that year. That was a special feeling," McGee said.

"I really realized after the season was over the impact of what had happened. We went on a trip to St. Thomas and Grenada, and we would be walking, and kids would see you from a block away and start jumping up and down. Everybody recognized you, and that's when I realized the impact of what had happened."

The good times were just beginning for McGee, who arrived in St. Louis as an unknown minor leaguer just at the moment Herzog was remaking the Cardinals into a team built on speed and defense.

McGee was on the Yankees' 40-man roster but was outrighted back to the minor leagues in October of 1981. That made McGee available on waivers to all of the major league clubs, and the Cardinals were among those interested.

"We had good reports on him, and we were afraid somebody else would take him before we would have a chance to claim him," Herzog said. "We called the Yankees and agreed to a trade—McGee for Bob Sykes."

It was a deal that later angered Yankees owner George Steinbrenner, who complained that the Cardinals had stolen McGee from him. Even though they were technically under no obligation to do so, after McGee had done so well for them, the Cardinals agreed to calm Steinbrenner down by "selling" two of their top prospects to the Yankees. Both shortstop Bobby Meacham and outfielder Stan Javier played several years in the major leagues.

The Cardinals got their first in-person look at McGee in spring training of 1982 and thought he looked promising. He was sent to Triple A Louisville to open the season, but when David Green got hurt in May, McGee was recalled to take his place. Nobody expected him to be anything more than a temporary fill-in, but he was determined to stay a bit longer.

McGee hit .296, drove in 56 runs, and added 25 stolen bases. He also quickly won over Cardinals fans with his shy demeanor, almost looking ashamed as he walked up to bat.

"He would get three hits a night and cry when he made an out," Herzog said. "He didn't swing at many strikes, but he really had a year."

The year continued in the playoffs and World Series. After batting .308 in the three-game sweep of the Braves, McGee hit .240 in the

World Series with five RBIs. He stole two bases and scored a team-high six runs.

That was an indication of how good McGee was going to be in a career that included winning the MVP award in 1985, the same year he won the first of his two National League batting titles.

"He could do everything," said teammate Bob Forsch. "And he never said anything boastful. It was like he was surprised he was that good."

McGee was eased into his transition to the major leagues with the help of an older and wiser veteran, Ozzie Smith. McGee actually lived with Smith for part of that year, and Smith was a guiding influence on McGee that McGee remembers to this day. He planned to be there in Cooperstown in July 2002 to honor his friend as he was inducted into the Hall of Fame.

McGee remembered everything Smith had done for him when another rookie—Vince Coleman—came up to the Cardinals in 1985. McGee tried to return Smith's favor by taking Coleman under his wing.

"I watched everything he did, and I did it. I don't know what would have happened to me if it weren't for Willie McGee," Coleman said. "I had talent, but so did a lot of other guys. I was fast and could steal bases in the minors. He taught me how to steal in the majors, how to read the pitcher."

Coleman was so wrapped up in honoring McGee during his retirement ceremony that Cardinals announcer Jack Buck had to almost wrestle him off the podium.

"Willie McGee played the game as it should be played. He played offense, defense, could steal bases—and he played hard every day," said Smith.

Another speaker that day was Sykes, who acknowledged that the trade that sent McGee from the Yankees to the Cardinals helped both players become famous.

"Personally, and I mean this from the bottom of my heart, it will be an honor for the rest of my life to be known in baseball as the player traded for Willie McGee," he told the crowd.

McGee was the league's Gold Glove center fielder in 1983, 1985, and 1986, and he added a second batting title in 1990. It would be an odd accomplishment for McGee, because he did not finish the season in St. Louis.

McGee spent seven-plus seasons with the Cardinals, and most fans thought he would never play for another team.

In 1990, Tony LaRussa's Oakland A's were one of baseball's dominant teams and were looking to add more offense to a lineup that included both Mark McGwire and Jose Canseco. While the Cardinals were on a West Coast road trip, McGee was traded to the A's. St. Louis' fans never got a chance to say good-bye.

The A's coasted to the World Series but were upset in a four-game sweep by Lou Piniella's Cincinnati Reds.

McGee was born in San Francisco, and after playing just 29 regular-season games with the A's, he signed with the San Francisco Giants as a free agent during that off-season.

McGee played four seasons with the Giants, the last of which was injury filled. During his time in San Francisco, he played for Dusty Baker. Baker called the 1993 team his closest unit.

"That was my first year, and the players were a great mix. It's hard to find a group like that again," Baker said. "We had Willie McGee and other players who were real warriors who played the game smart. It makes it easier on the manager because McGee and those guys lead on the field and in the clubhouse."

McGee appeared in only 45 games because of a torn Achilles tendon in 1994, and in 1995 he signed with Boston's Triple A Pawtucket farm club in June. He appeared in Boston's Division Series loss to Cleveland. It looked like his career was drawing to a close.

Then, his old team, his true baseball love, called and wanted him back.

McGee returned to the Cardinals from 1996 to 1999, twice hitting over .300. He got his 2,000th hit on August 8, 1996.

In a bit of irony, McGee had gotten his first hit against another former Cardinal, Al Hrabosky.

"I got to start against Al Hrabosky [in his second big-league game] so that was a big thrill," McGee said. "It was on TBS so my family could see me. It was with the bases loaded. Everybody knows Al;

he's competitive. It was a battle. It was 3–2, and he kept coming right at me. That's Al Hrabosky, he's very aggressive as a ballplayer and a pitcher. That's why he was so good."

In his first game back in St. Louis after five years, on a frigid Opening Night game, McGee pinch hit in the ninth inning and lined a game-winning walk-off home run. Smith was in the broadcast booth, leading the cheers.

McGee was back, and the fans loved it. He was swarmed by media representatives in the clubhouse after the game.

He was as humble as he had been on the May day in 1982 when he reported to the major leagues for the first time. And he hasn't changed in retirement, either, trying not to take credit for his accomplishments and trying to live a routine life of a father with four girls.

Someday, McGee said, he will come back to St. Louis, but his family is uppermost in his mind at this point in his life, keeping him from straying too far from his home in Hurcules, California.

"You just have to transform into your next life [after baseball]," said McGee, the son of a minister. "You have to find things to do to fill up that space—the hours you spent playing baseball. Most of it is family stuff."

McGee's four daughters are ages 19, 14, 12, and 8. The former superstar is now just a dad.

"I take them back and forth to school; one is running track, and two are playing softball," McGee said. "I thought I would have a lot more time on my hands, but I really don't. I really don't have the time to do what I want to do."

While McGee is comfortable in retirement, he says he dreaded the end of his magnificent career.

"Before I retired I was scared," he said. "I had played baseball for so long, I really wondered what I was going to do. You hear stories about guys going astray and all that kind of stuff. But nothing like that has happened to me.

"I actually miss baseball less than I thought I would. You realize when you get to be a certain age that you just physically can't play anymore. You adjust to it. I miss the camaraderie; I miss batting practice and shagging fly balls. I don't miss the stress, and I find other ways to replace the competition."

Can you imagine Willie McGee swinging a golf club?

"Yes, I play golf. I'm doing what I have to do now. I wish I could do what I want to do. I would be playing golf every day."

Baseball is still in his routine, from Little League to the minors.

"I go out and work with Little League teams or college teams; I do things at church and try to help other families. It fills a void in my life," he said.

McGee went to spring training with the Giants in Arizona for a second year in 2002, working entirely in the minor league camp.

He also is in his second year working for the Giants as a roving instructor in the minors during the season, working seven days a month. He works on teaching base running, playing the outfield, and bunting.

"I've observed a lot, but just because you played for a long time and had some success doesn't mean you can teach," McGee said. "I talk to guys about the mental aspect of the game more than anything. I really find it more rewarding. That's why I didn't go to big-league camp.

"It's like your kids asking you questions. These kids are just being raised in baseball. You don't know what to expect."

Cardinals fans can expect to see McGee again, maybe in a new stadium. But they must be patient.

"Someday, I would like to come back to St. Louis and coach," McGee said. "I'm a Cardinal. I'd love to come back one day. But right now my family comes first."

No one who knows McGee is surprised.

11 | Ken Oberkfell

Ever since he left his home in Maryville, Illinois, when he was 19 years old to begin playing baseball in the Cardinals' farm system, Ken Oberkfell has never had a job that was not related to baseball.

Asked what he would be doing now if he wasn't involved in baseball, Oberkfell had to pause for a long while before he could come up with an answer. "I don't know," he said. "Maybe, 'You want fries with that Big Mac?' All I've ever done is baseball."

Oberkfell had a 16-year major league career, retiring in 1992, and after sitting out two years to play golf and relax, he got back into baseball in 1995 as the manager of an independent team in the Northeast League, in Sullivan County, New York.

The 2002 season found Oberkfell in Port St. Lucie, Florida, beginning his eighth year of managing in the minor leagues, guiding the New York Mets' team in the Class A Florida State League.

In between his first and latest jobs, Oberkfell spent a year managing another independent team in Elmira, New York; three years managing Piedmont in the Class A South Atlantic League, a Phillies' affiliate; one year managing Clearwater in the Florida State League for the Phillies; and a year managing Capital City (Columbia, South Carolina) in the South Atlantic League for the Mets.

"I love it," Oberkfell said. "At the end of my playing career I was more of a utility guy, and I would sit on the bench and think to myself, 'What would I do here if I was managing?' I knew I wanted to stay in the game.

"I really enjoy working with the young kids, and the real satisfaction comes when you see them succeed and get to the major leagues and have some success. You like to think you maybe had a little to do with it."

Almost all of the good young players now on the Philadelphia Phillies played for Oberkfell along the way, including shortstop Jimmy Rollins, the runner-up to the Cardinals' Albert Pujols in the NL Rookie of the Year voting in 2001, and pitcher Brandon Duckworth.

As a minor league manager, especially when he is working with kids barely out of high school, Oberkfell knows there is much more to his job description than merely running a game and deciding when to change pitchers or send up a pinch-hitter.

All he has to do is remember what those days—now longer ago than he would like to admit—were like for him, and it is easy to relate to the problems and frustrations his players are experiencing.

"I don't think when I left home to go to extended spring training with the Cardinals I had ever been out of the Maryville area," Oberkfell said. "You [the manager] almost become like a father figure to these kids. You have to keep them positive, with an upbeat attitude. They will get homesick, but I tell them my door is always open."

Oberkfell likely enjoys his job because he has the proper perspective and understanding of what playing in the minor leagues is all about. He knows the majority of the players he is managing will never play in the majors, but he knows his job is to develop as many of those players into potential major leaguers as possible.

"My big thing is when guys get frustrated I tell them as long as you have a uniform on, you have a chance," Oberkfell said. "I was a free-agent signee; I wasn't drafted. I was not a big bonus baby. But I was determined, and I had great desire. They were going to have to tear the uniform off me. I tell these guys, 'Let the organization tell you when you're done. This is the greatest game in the world. Play it as long as you can.'"

Especially this year, in the Florida State League, Oberkfell doesn't even mind the bus rides. His longest trip is 4 hours, down from the 13-hour trip last year to go from Columbia, South Carolina, to Lakewood, New Jersey.

"The bus trips I really remember were when I was playing in Arkansas and we had to go from Little Rock to El Paso, Texas," Oberkfell said. "I remember thinking, 'This dang state is so big, how could anyone want to live here.' And now I've been living in Texas for 12 years."

Even though he loves the minor leagues, it is no secret that Oberkfell's goal is to one day make it back to the major leagues, as either a coach or a manager.

"You just have to pay your dues and see what happens," he said. "I did it as a player; now I'm doing it as a manager."

Like many players who came before him and those who followed him to the majors years later, Oberkfell gives much of the credit for his reaching the major leagues to Cardinals' guru George Kissell. Once in the majors, the credit for his success went to Whitey Herzog, Oberkfell said.

"George really took me under his wing," Oberkfell said. "He was the guy who taught me the most about how to play the game the right way. When I got to the majors, I loved playing for Whitey. He was the best manager I ever played for. The greatest thing about Whitey was the way he handled each individual player. He knew when to pat a guy on the back and when to kick him in the butt. He made all of the extra guys feel like they were important too.

"He tried to put guys in positions where they had the greatest chances of being successful. I try to do that too, and most of that I learned from Whitey."

When he first came up to the Cardinals, Oberkfell played second base. With Tom Herr also advancing through the system, however, Herzog knew he had to make a decision that would allow him to get both Oberkfell and Herr in the lineup. The solution came when he was able to trade Ken Reitz and Leon Durham to the Cubs for Bruce Sutter. He was able to put Herr at second and move Oberkfell to third.

When Ozzie Smith was added to the lineup a year later, the infield was set. Oberkfell doesn't want to brag, but he thinks the foursome of Keith Hernandez, Herr, Smith, and himself was pretty good.

"Arguably I think it was the best infield in the game," Oberkfell said. "I know there have been some good ones, but all of us I think were good enough to win a Gold Glove. The special thing about that ballclub was that we were a close-knit group. We all hung out together. We also were pretty good."

In 1982, Oberkfell wasn't worried about his future or any long-term goals.

"The only thing we were concerned about was trying to win a world championship," he said. "It doesn't seem like it was 20 years ago. It seems like only yesterday to me. Growing up as a Cardinals fan, and then having the opportunity to play for the team, and win a world championship, it was like a dream."

Oberkfell's personal highlight came in the National League play-offs, in the second game against Atlanta, when he delivered the game-winning hit in the bottom of the ninth inning.

"Gene Garber was pitching, and Bruce Benedict was catching," Oberkfell said. "I had always hit Garber pretty well, and I remember hitting a ball that just went foul. I turned back to Bruce and said, 'You still going to pitch to me?' I think Dane Iorg was on deck. He said yeah, and then I got the hit.

"I remember being back in the dugout and the fans were cheering like crazy, and Frank Coppenbarger [one of the assistant equipment managers] kept saying, 'The fans want you to come back out.' That was a great moment."

Another great moment came a few days later, in the seventh game of the World Series.

"I had been pinch hit for, so I was in the dugout, and I was more nervous sitting there than I would have been playing," Oberkfell said.

"We had just had twins born in September, and I remember being home that morning and the only thing I was thinking about was getting to the ballpark.

"It all came down to that one game, whether we would be the world champions or the National League champions. It was probably about noon when I got to the park—for a night game—and a bunch of guys were already there."

His love of the Cardinals, and the success he had in St. Louis, made it a very difficult moment for Oberkfell when, less than two years later, he was traded to the Atlanta Braves.

"If it hadn't been that we had Terry Pendleton in the minor leagues and playing real well, we would not have traded him," Herzog said. "He was a really good defensive third baseman and a really good guy on the ballclub. I really enjoyed managing him. Actually, if we had not had Tom Herr come up when he did, Obie could have stayed at second base and done a great job there."

As hard as it was for Oberkfell to accept the trade, he realized later that it turned out to be a blessing.

"In a way it was the best thing that happened to me," Oberkfell said. "I got to play in Atlanta and prolong my career. Unfortunately, I was with the Braves before they started winning all those games. I enjoyed my time there."

When he signed as a free agent with the Astros in 1990, Oberkfell decided to move to the Houston area, and that is still where he makes his off-season home. He has remarried, and he and his wife, Tina, have three children. Oberkfell has three older children from his first marriage.

"The tough part of the game is being away from home," he said. "I don't think a lot of people understand that, and in the minor leagues, you certainly aren't doing it for the money. It's good they can come visit in the summer and see a new place, and then at least you get the winter off to spend with them. That's a good thing."

When he is home in the winter, especially on days when he can't go golfing, Oberkfell will occasionally pop the tape of the 1982 World Series into his VCR and sit down and watch it.

"Tina will come up and say, 'Are you watching that again?' but it's special to me," Oberkfell said. "A lot of great players never have that opportunity, to play in the World Series. And it was a great World Series. Except for the birth of my children, it was maybe the highlight of my life."

12 | Darrell Porter

Darrell Porter had been involved in professional baseball for so long, he was looking forward to seeing the game on another level after he retired—watching his three children play.

When he went out to watch their games, however, "I was appalled," he said.

What Porter saw was a far different environment from the one he had grown up with in Oklahoma. As he became more familiar with the current state of youth sports in the United States, he realized that what he was watching was a problem not just in his hometown of Lee's Summit, Missouri, but a nationwide concern.

"People were expecting their kids to be perfect," Porter said. "There were people yelling and screaming at the kids. These people were forgetting that even big leaguers don't make all the plays. People were beating up on the coaches and the umpires."

Porter couldn't believe what he was seeing, how parents could act that way, and even the kids themselves, yelling and criticizing their teammates for making a mistake that he considered just part of the game. What he didn't know was that almost at the same time, a friend of his was also becoming aware of the increasing problem with youth sports and was determined to try to do something about it.

Bill Stutz, who had been friends with Porter for nearly a decade, was an area director for the Fellowship of Christian Athletes. Like Porter, he loved sports and wanted to give back to his local sports organizations but could not believe the atmosphere he thought was poisoning the games for the kids.

"He was tired of seeing what he saw out there," Porter said. "He was complaining about it, and his wife invoked their no-whining rule: if you are going to bring up a problem, you can't do it without also bringing a solution to the problem."

The solution turned out to be a new company, Enjoy the Game, which Stutz founded. Porter has been working with him for almost two years. The basic goal of the company is to get its educational program into the hands of as many schools and athletic organizations as possible, refocusing the attention of parents, coaches, and the players themselves on the sheer joy of playing the game.

"What it teaches is respect for your teammates or peers, the coaches or teachers, and to respect authority and the rules and to do what's right," Porter said. "One of the reasons why it is so effective is that it is so simple. In all of our venues, we put up banners and signs to remind people that 'this is an Enjoy the Game facility.' We want the environment to be positive and encouraging."

The program has now been adopted by schools and organizations in 16 states and is continuing to expand. In the summer of 2002, the McDonald's restaurants in the Denver area were conducting a test market of the program. The company was sponsoring the program at area schools, where youngsters were taught the program's principles in four sessions. After that, any youngster caught acting out one of the principles was given a gift certificate for a free Happy Meal at McDonald's.

Porter's goal, and Stutz's as well, is to return the atmosphere surrounding youth sports back to what it was decades ago.

"You know I really don't remember many of my teachers from school, but I remember every coach I ever had," Porter said. "And I don't really remember them teaching me anything about baseball. But I remember them always being positive and presenting an encouraging environment. I think that really had as much as anything to do with bringing me from the Little League fields of Oklahoma to the World Series at Busch Stadium."

Reaching the 1982 World Series allowed Porter to finally enjoy the game of baseball in St. Louis after a frustrating start to his career with the Cardinals, signed away from Kansas City as a free agent, the first significant move Whitey Herzog made after becoming the team's manager.

Herzog's master plan, after signing Porter, was to move popular catcher Ted Simmons to first base and shift Keith Hernandez to left field. He still thinks that would have worked out fine, except Simmons had second thoughts about the position change and asked to be traded. Herzog then worked out the Milwaukee trade that sent Simmons to the Brewers and forced Porter into becoming his unpopular replacement.

"I'm kind of a sensitive guy, and I've always loved the fans," Porter said. "It was a hard situation for me; it was real difficult. I was still trying to recover from drug and alcohol abuse at the same time. I know there were a lot of people cheering for me, but it really is amazing how all you hear are the boos. My wife, Deanne, and I were not sure we wanted to stay in St. Louis when we got there. But it grew on us."

That was no doubt in part helped by Porter's performance in the 1982 playoff series against the Braves and in the World Series against the Brewers. He was named the MVP of both series, hitting .556 in the playoffs and delivering a key hit in Game 7 of the World Series.

"It had not been the greatest year I've ever had, but I got hot at the end of the season, and that carried over into the playoffs and World Series and I did well," Porter said. "There were quite a few guys who did well. There were several guys who could have won the MVP."

It was no surprise to Herzog, who had managed Porter with the Royals, that Porter came through when the games mattered the most.

"All I know is he won two titles with me in Kansas City," Herzog said. "He just had a knack for playing baseball. He was the kind of guy who could hit .220 and help a team just about as much as a guy who hit .300 and didn't pull the ball. When he got a hit, everybody advanced two bases, and when he made an out, they advanced one base. He could do more a lot of times making an out than a guy who hit a clunker to left field.

"Obviously a base hit is better than an out, but what it meant was that the next guy hitting after Porter didn't have to get a hit to drive in a run.

"He also had a knack of knowing how his pitchers got people out. He didn't catch as much against the hitter as he caught to the strength of the pitcher. He really knew how to handle a pitcher.

"I managed him for eight years, and we won five division titles, two pennants, and a World Series. It really wasn't until we won the Series and he won the MVP in the playoffs and Series, though, that people in St. Louis got to know him and started to take a liking to him."

Porter stayed in St. Louis through the 1985 season, then played the final two years of his 17-year major league career in Texas, retiring after the 1987 season.

He admits it took him time to settle into life after baseball, a problem he thinks was not unique.

"I didn't know what to expect, and it was difficult at times," Porter said. "It's a funny world we live in in pro sports, and it's not very realistic. A lot of us had never done anything in our lives except play sports. Finding your purpose and goals after you leave the game can take a while."

Porter tried several businesses, never feeling 100 percent comfortable in any of them. He bought and sold real estate, then he got into the antiques business. He designed and built a Little League baseball complex in Independence, and he coached the teams for his three children. His daughter, Lindsey, is now 20 and a student at Baylor University. His son Jeff is a junior in high school, and he has another son, Ryan, who is 13. Porter also is doing some broadcasting work, calling high school basketball and baseball games in the Kansas City area, and was included in the group of broadcasters working Royals games in 2002.

Both of his boys are playing baseball and have shown some promise as left-handed pitchers, their dad said.

"I think if they show any promise at all they will get a chance to prove themselves someday," Porter said.

What he saw coaching and watching his children play, plus his conversations with Stutz over the years, was what convinced Porter the best job he could have is the one he is doing now—trying to change the world of youth sports.

He knows it isn't an easy assignment, and he and Stutz are comfortable measuring their success with small victories. Porter also is glad when opportunities come around for him to do public speaking appearances, giving him a chance to share his faith, tell the story of his life, and talk about many of the bad choices he made and how his life could have turned out much differently had he not gotten the help he needed and become a Christian.

"I could be dead or in jail," Porter admits. "I tell my story about how I got involved with bad choices and how I've been able to recover. I've got three great kids and a wonderful wife. I'm very lucky."

Whenever he signs an autograph, Porter also writes Prov. 3:5–6, referring to his favorite Bible verses, Proverbs, Chapter 3, verses five and six. The verses read, "Trust in the Lord with all your heart. Lean not unto your own understanding. In all your ways acknowledge Him, and He shall direct your path."

Porter said the reasons he always cites that scripture passage with his autograph are because it helps him with his goal of honoring and acknowledging God in everything he does and because it is his favorite verse, one that has personally meant a lot to him over the years.

"I have discovered that life is not always easy," Porter said, "and we all are confronted at times with things that we don't understand. We wonder why such things would happen to us or others we love. This verse tells us that if we have a personal relationship with God, and trust in Him, we can know that no matter what happens to us

God is in control. If we stay faithful to Him, He will guide us through our lives, even our toughest storms."

Porter has some goals and plans for the future, but for now, he says, he wants to spend as much time as possible with his kids.

"My family is more important than anything," he said. "I'm very comfortable where I am right now."

Porter has the trophy that he won for being the MVP of the 1982 World Series proudly displayed in his house, but he needed all of his family, love to get over the loss of another prized possession, the red 1982 Pontiac Trans Am he also received for being the Series MVP.

Porter did not drive the car much; it had only 34,000 miles on it when one day a couple of years ago he let his daughter, Lindsey, drive it to high school.

"She totaled it," Porter said. "Luckily she wasn't hurt. I've still got it; it's parked out on my father-in-law's farm. The whole front end is torn up. I'm still going to try to get it fixed someday."

Editor's note: On August 5, 2002, Darrell Porter was found dead beside his car in a park in suburban Kansas City. Authorities said Porter's car had apparently become stuck against a tree stump, and they speculated that he died while attempting to push the car off the stump.

13 | Mike Ramsey

Mike Ramsey can be excused if it takes him a minute to recite the list of stops he has made over his 12-year career of managing in the minor leagues.

After all, he is now in Hagerstown, Maryland, managing in his fourth organization and has never been at any city longer than two years.

The word he uses to describe his career thus far is *odyssey*. But he quickly adds, "I've moved around, but I've got no regrets. It's been a lot of fun."

His first stop was in Springfield, Illinois, where he was hired to manage the Cardinals' Class A team in 1990 by former player development director Ted Simmons. That assignment came two years after Ramsey's playing career ended, when he decided it was time to get a job and baseball was what he knew best.

"I was out of the game living in St. Louis and basically didn't do anything," Ramsey said. "I had a little gig with a local cable television show for about six months, and I really had to make a decision what I wanted to do. I had been talking to Ted about getting back into it, and he offered me a chance, and I took it."

From Springfield, Ramsey moved on to Savannah, Georgia; St. Petersburg, Florida; and Little Rock, Arkansas, before he was fired by the Cardinals, essentially because he did not immediately inform the front office the night Dmitri Young went charging into the stands after a harassing fan during a game in Wichita, Kansas

Ramsey intended to make that call the following day, after returning to Little Rock, but the report of the incident got back to St. Louis from the media before Ramsey called, and that upset his bosses.

"It was a messy situation," Ramsey said. "What I should have done was called right away, and I didn't. I was remiss in my duties there. I couldn't have controlled what actually happened, but I should have had a better handle on Dmitri."

Ramsey learned from that experience, and he has also been able to absorb knowledge and become a better manager every place he has been during his career.

He moved to the San Diego Padres' organization from St. Louis, managing in Clinton, Iowa, and Mobile, Alabama, before moving up to manage the Triple A team in Las Vegas. When he was fired again, he landed what he thought would be a dream job with the expansion Tampa Bay Devil Rays, the team closest to his off-season home in Largo, Florida.

Ramsey spent two years managing the Devil Rays' Double A team in Orlando, but then he was fired again, at the end of last season.

Now he has moved on to the Giants' system, taking over the Hagerstown Suns in the Class A South Atlantic League.

"I really had no preconceived notions of what this career was going to be like," Ramsey said. "Up until I was out of the game, I really had not planned or thought I wanted to stay in the game. I've enjoyed most of it, except for a few difficulties with some higher-ups in the various organizations.

"It usually takes a couple of years for me to tick somebody off. Most of the things that have got me in trouble had nothing to do with baseball on the field, such as the problem with Dmitri."

The longer he has managed, however, the more Ramsey has come to understand that there is greater responsibility placed on a minor league manager than simply controlling the game on the field. This is especially true when he is managing younger and less experienced players, such as he is doing again this year.

"You have to keep a finger on everybody," he said. "It took me a little while to realize that you don't treat these guys like big-league players. You've got to monitor them a little more closely."

He has also learned that that tighter control applies even when the game is in progress.

"That was another mistake I made, not realizing that they may not know what to do in certain situations," Ramsey said. "They need to be told even the smallest thing that you think they ought to already know. You have to tell them what you want them to do."

Ramsey has had other rough moments as a manager. One of his pitchers was killed in a car accident when he was managing Springfield in 1993. He also managed Mike Darr, the Padres' outfielder killed in spring training in 2002 in another accident.

Another night he will never forget came when he was managing Springfield and went out to argue an umpire's call with a dip of chewing tobacco in his mouth.

"I was really hot, and that usually only happens about once a year," Ramsey said. "My spittle started going all over the man. I got him so bad. He was covered. It was right before they started banning chewing tobacco in the minors. I got run [out of the game] pretty quick. I did apologize to him the next day."

The longer he has managed, and at the three different minor league levels, the more Ramsey has realized it doesn't really make any difference what level he is managing; the game is the same, and he can have just as much fun in Single A as he can have in Triple A.

He also has come to realize that managing younger players at the Class A level might actually be more important to the long-term success of a major league franchise than managing at the Triple A level.

"I used to think I wanted to manage at the highest level possible, but I don't really feel that way anymore," Ramsey said. "I've changed my perspective. The biggest thing you have to realize about managing at this level is that what almost all of these kids need the most is experience playing the game. There is no substitute for getting games under your belt. These guys have never played a 140-game season before. It's different learning how to do that."

Like almost all of Whitey's former players who have gone on to become minor league managers, Ramsey admits that much of what he learned about how to be a manager came from Whitey Herzog.

"I had plenty of time to watch [during] the five years I was there," Ramsey said. "It says a lot about Whitey and the kind of manager he was that so many of us feel that way. Simmons taught me a lot about handling a pitching staff my first couple of years. I learned a lot from him too."

Even though he jokes about sitting on the bench during his career in St. Louis, Ramsey wouldn't trade those memories for anything. His personal highlight, of course, came when the Cardinals won the 1982 World Series.

Ramsey got the chance to be more involved that season than he might otherwise have been because of a hamstring injury to Ozzie Smith that sidelined the starting shortstop for 14 consecutive games during the September pennant run. Ramsey played errorless ball for those 14 games, and in one particular stretch, when the Cardinals played five games in a 48-hour span against the Mets, he was the only Cardinal to play every inning of every game. The Cardinals won all five games.

"You're talking about a utility infielder going into the lineup at that time of year and playing the way he played; it was unbelievable," Herzog said. "But those are the kinds of things that happen to you when you are doing well. He was unheralded, but he did a hell of a job. Everybody thought when Ozzie got hurt that we were done, but that wasn't the case."

Ramsey enjoyed getting that chance to play.

"I had come up behind [Garry] Templeton, and I really didn't think I was going to be a big leaguer," Ramsey said. "But I managed to make a spot for myself for a few years.

"Whitey turned our fortunes around and got us to the World Series. That really set up everything I do. Being able to be in St. Louis around that time gave me the chance to put some money away and be able to work in the minor leagues without really having to worry too much about the money."

The biggest worry Ramsey has these days is that he is spending too much time away from home and his wife, Merle, and their two sons, Matt, 13, and Jordan, 8. It was easy for them to travel to wherever he was working when the boys were younger, but now that they are in school and involved in sports, it is harder for them to be gone for long periods of time.

Their absence is hard on Ramsey.

"I looked into doing some other things last winter and thought long and hard about it," Ramsey said. "I was thinking maybe about going back to school. Some guys I know operate baseball schools and give private lessons, and they make a living doing that.

"But I don't know what else I could do where I would have as much fun."

Every time one of his former players makes it to the major leagues and has some success, Ramsey likes to think he played at least a small part in that player's development. Most of the young players on the Padres came through him, and so did the Mets' Joe McEwing, when he was in the Cardinals' system.

And as long as his love for family doesn't create a change in his life, he plans to keep on managing for as long as possible.

"Baseball is where I'm happiest," he said. "It's what I know more than anything."

14 | Lonnie Smith

onnie Smith wants to make one point very clear. He isn't bitter toward baseball. At this particular moment in his life, he is dedicating himself to being the best husband and father he can be, and that means he cannot let himself get caught up in any of his past problems.

Was he bitter in the past? Absolutely.

"What really held me together late in my career was I met my new wife and she was a big inspiration to me," Smith said. "She kept me in line. There were so many times I was frustrated and thought about doing some of the stupidest things in life. I was not on drugs, but I was acting like I was."

Smith's problems in baseball began with the Cardinals in 1982, even though that was perhaps the greatest year of his career, finishing second in the National League MVP race to Atlanta's Dale Murphy. That was the year his drug problem began, which was the major source of his problems for most of the next decade.

Smith, of course, was not alone in his struggles with drug addiction. Drugs were a major problem in the early eighties, and investigations by Major League Baseball and the FBI led to a series of trials in

Pittsburgh in 1985. Eventually seven drug dealers either pleaded guilty or were convicted of selling cocaine to major league players.

He was involved in the drug trials in Pittsburgh, testifying as the number one witness for the prosecution. Even though he was granted immunity from federal prosecution, he still was the first person disciplined by Commissioner Peter Ueberroth after the trials were over. He was fined, suspended, and ordered to perform 100 hours of community service, even though all he had done was agree to whatever the commissioner asked him to do.

After suffering through those problems, Smith believes he was one of the players affected by collusion in the mideighties and that his team at the time, the Kansas City Royals, attempted to blackball him from baseball, labeling him as a player with a bad attitude.

Smith admits he was so upset and angered that he actually went out and bought a gun.

"I contemplated going to Kansas City and shooting a couple of people," Smith admitted in a quiet, calm voice. "I blamed them for everything. It was the only reason I ever had to buy a gun."

Luckily, Smith never acted on his anger but instead let time try to heal those wounds. Still, almost eight years removed from his last game as a major leaguer, Smith believes one person—former Kansas City and current Atlanta general manager John Schuerholz—was responsible for most of his problems toward the end of his career.

"I have never hated anyone as much as I hated him," Smith said. "I don't like the man."

As luck would have it, after Smith struggled to find a job before making it back to the major leagues with Atlanta, what happened? Schuerholz left Kansas City to become general manager of the Braves. More troubles for Smith followed, and finally, when he walked away from the game in spring training of 1995, he was ready to move on with his life.

"I can't complain about what I went through, because half of it was caused by myself, but the other half I thought was taken away from me," Smith said. "That's life. I played with a lot of great Hall of Famers. I played in five World Series, won three and lost two.

"I'm happy, and that's all I ever wanted to be. I still miss the game, but I'm happy the way things are now. I can't stay bitter the rest of my life; it wears on my family."

Smith's family now includes his two grown children from his first marriage, wife Dorothy, and their three daughters, ages nine, seven, and three. The couple met in 1988 when they were introduced by a friend of one of Smith's cousins, who had come from Wisconsin to visit Smith when the Braves were playing in Chicago.

The family moved to Fayette County, Georgia, just south of Atlanta, in 1990. They now live in what Smith describes as a comfortable house situated on two acres. Baseball did afford him the ability to stay home and take care of his daughters and not have to work on a daily basis.

"When I called it quits I made up my mind I was going to be a father and a husband," Smith said. "With my first two kids, I didn't get a chance to spend much time with them except in the winter. I was dedicated to do that, and I haven't regretted it. I was fortunate that I met a banker who helped take care of my money. I was able to set up trust funds for all of my kids.

"We don't live very high, but we're comfortable."

Other than driving his kids to their various activities, Smith spends most of his time these days working around the yard. His task on this particular day is to patch an approximately 20-square-foot section of grass.

"I've always enjoyed working in the yard," Smith said. "I grew up cutting grass and weeding flower beds. I don't mind doing it. It's my house, and I like to keep it looking nice."

Smith's one attempt to set up a business near the end of his career involved a landscaping company, but the company failed when his partner took off with the $50,000 Smith had invested as bond money. Smith hasn't seen him or talked to him since. In the future, he admits, there is a possibility that he would like to get back into baseball, working as a coach, especially in the lower levels of the minor leagues, where he thinks he could help with the development of young players.

Those thoughts have been placed on hold for the time being, however, until his children are grown.

"This is where I need to be and where I need to stay," Smith said.

He is content to stay home with his family, work on his own yard, and not think very often about his baseball past—unless someone else brings it up. He is not recognized as much in the Atlanta area as he would be in Philadelphia or St. Louis, he says, probably in part because he is heavier now than during his playing days.

"I had my annual physical, and the doctor said everything was fine and I was healthy," Smith said. "The last eight years have taken a toll on my waistline, since I basically stopped working out. I know I could stand to drop 30 pounds."

During most of his career, Smith weighed about 175 pounds. The doctor weighed him at 239 during his physical in April 2002. A calm and content Smith is even OK with that.

"I don't like to be that size, but it is what I am, so I have to accept it," Smith said.

Accept is also a good word to describe Smith's response to his past baseball problems, at least the ones that he believes he brought on himself because of his drug use. He blames nobody but himself for that, but he also believes he is sometimes mislabeled as the cause of all of baseball's drug problems in the eighties, when he actually played only a very small role.

"The sad part is that most people don't know the whole story," Smith said. "Most of the media I spoke to all thought I was only one mistake behind Steve Howe. The truth is I went into rehab on my own; I was never arrested. Everything I did in the Pittsburgh trials I was asked to do by Major League Baseball.

"What a lot of people assumed is that I didn't have to testify. The front office of the Cardinals, the league president, and the commissioner all told me to tell the truth. Maybe I hurt the images of a couple of people, but I had nothing to hide."

Smith talks openly and honestly about his problems with taking drugs.

"I first experimented with it in Venezuela when I was playing winter ball," he said. "I enjoyed it, but it wasn't like it was readily available. Then I got a little cocky and started experimenting more and more frequently. It came back to haunt me, because then I started wanting it all the time, and I didn't think about anything else.

"After 1982 I started getting stuff in the mail through the winter, and in 1983 I was involved pretty bad. I couldn't function as a husband, a father, or a player. I was rushing back to my room, locking the door, and doing it. I was constantly doing it until I ran out, and then I wanted to go out and do more."

What Smith was doing was snorting cocaine up his nose.

"I wasn't eating or sleeping. I got down to 160 pounds, and I had a 28-inch waistline, which is the size I was in junior high school. I was very weak; I was constantly sweating and constantly nervous. Everything was crashing down on me. I would go three days without sleeping, then try to go out and play."

Finally one day, as he was taking the team bus from the hotel in Philadelphia to Veterans Stadium, Smith knew he had to have help. He walked in and told manager Whitey Herzog what was going on. Herzog told Smith to go sleep in the training room and the team would make the necessary arrangements to get help.

Smith flew with the Cardinals to Chicago after the game, then the next day he flew on to St. Louis, where he was admitted to the Hyland Center. He spent five weeks going through the rehabilitation program.

"If you make the decision yourself to go through that type of program, they say the chance of relapsing is much smaller," Smith said. "You have to follow through on your aftercare. You still have moments. It's kind of like stopping smoking. I stopped smoking cigarettes about four years ago. Sometimes now I will crave a cigarette, but I know I can't start or I will be right back where I was."

Smith was able to put his drug problems behind him when he returned to the Cardinals, only to have them come up again a year later when the FBI initiated an investigation and made various arrests and baseball needed Smith to testify for the prosecution.

"The first step in recovery is admitting you have a problem," Smith said. "The second step is talking about it, and you have to tell the truth and deal with the problem. I really think going through everything I went through made me a better person, because it made me more open and honest."

Smith was amazed that there was no negative response to his problems when he rejoined the Cardinals. "People accepted me back," he said. "The fans were terrific."

Then came the day in 1985 when Smith's world turned again, when the Cardinals traded him to Kansas City, opening up left field for a rookie called up from Louisville, Vince Coleman.

"I actually thought about giving up baseball," Smith said. "I didn't think I could go anyplace better."

It turned out Smith was right, only he had no idea at the time how bad things were going to get.

"There was a different atmosphere about baseball in the American League," Smith said. "It was a different way of life. There were great players and good organizations, but everything was different."

Smith describes his entire experience with the Royals as a nightmare. It was the only time in his career, he said, that when he went to find a place to live he was forced to pay all of the rent up front for the entire season.

After agreeing to testify in the drug trials, Smith found himself called into Ueberroth's office, along with his lawyer and agent. The commissioner told Smith that he wanted Smith's help in trying to get drugs out of baseball.

Smith flew to New York, paying his own expenses and those of his lawyer and agent, then went to Ueberroth's office for the meeting. After Smith was kept waiting, Ueberroth showed up and asked Smith only two questions—what do you think we could do to get rid of drugs in baseball, and another general question Smith can't remember.

"That was it," Smith said. "I spent all that money and went there for that. Why bother?"

Smith was in for another disappointment when his "penalty" was handed down by Ueberroth, even though he had never been told he was going to be disciplined by baseball for his testimony. There were organizations that wanted him to fight it, but the Royals' front office told him not to, and Smith agreed.

He had a relative in the police department in Spartanburg, South Carolina, where he was living at the time, and he set up various speeches for Smith before schools, clubs, and organizations to fulfill his community service requirement.

"I wouldn't have minded if I had been told what I was going to have to do," Smith said. "I knew I had made some mistakes, and I tried to correct them."

Just when he again thought all of his problems should be behind him, more trouble developed in 1986, which was the option year on his contract. Even though he was playing well, with an average close to .300, veteran Hal McRae came up to Smith one day and told him not to be surprised if he suddenly began playing a lot less often. It was because of the option in his contract, McRae said, noting that the Royals had done the same thing to him.

"The next thing I know, life was hell," Smith said. "They bought out the option, then tried to say they wanted to sign me for a lot less money, arguing that the buyout was part of the contract. I had a couple of other clubs interested, but they weren't going to pay more than Kansas City. I had to wait until May [in 1987] to re-sign, then they sent me to Triple A. When I came back up, I played only part time, and they released me at the end of the year."

Smith finally was able to catch on with the Braves, again through a minor league contract, and worked his way back up to the major leagues, becoming the comeback player of the year in 1989. He injured his leg, however, and that affected his playing time, and then his old boss from Kansas City, Schuerholz, arrived in Atlanta.

"I knew I would be moving on soon," Smith said.

Smith wound up in Pittsburgh and then Baltimore before calling it a career.

Luckily for Smith, that career included three-plus years in St. Louis, easily the best of times for him, highlighted by the 1982 world championship. Smith hit .307, led the league with 120 runs scored, hit eight home runs, drove in 69 runs, and stole 68 bases. Eight of the twenty-eight writers who voted for the MVP that year thought Smith deserved the award, and he did finish second in the balloting.

"What a leadoff man he was, and what a hard-nosed player," Herzog said. "He was one of the best I've ever seen at breaking up a double play. He had a hell of a year. He also was such an exciting player because he made so many mistakes on the bases. He was the best leadoff man I've ever seen in the National League because of the pitcher batting. If we could bunt the runner over, Lonnie would drive in those runs for us with two outs. He was always a tough out."

Smith admits 1982 was a magical year.

"Anything and everything that could go right went right," he said. "I played for a manager who let me play. I was reunited with Ozzie [Smith], who I had played with in Little League. We had a lot of great players, and it was a beautiful season."

That was a happy time for Smith, only he had no idea of the trials and tribulations that would be coming his way. With the ability now to put everything that has happened to him in perspective, Smith is glad he had had the good times, glad he survived the bad times, and glad to be where he is and the person he is at this point in his life.

"I always told myself and my family that when my career was over all I wanted to do was be normal and be happy," Smith said. "I can honestly say I'm happy."

15 | Ozzie Smith

Waiting for an expected telephone call can be excruciatingly painful. Knowing that when the telephone does ring, it could bring the news that you have been elected to the Hall of Fame makes that wait even more difficult.

Ozzie Smith knows what that wait is like.

Five years after his playing career ended—another seemingly long wait—Smith waited for the phone call from Jack O'Connell, the secretary of the Baseball Writers Association of America, on a January day in 2002. He had tried to prepare himself for the possibility that he might not be elected. After all, first-ballot selection is reserved for the best of the best. He wanted to be able to deal with his possible failure to receive the votes necessary for election in a calm and collected manner.

That wasn't necessary. When the telephone finally rang at his home in St. Albans, Missouri, Smith was told he had been elected to the Hall of Fame with 91.7 percent of the vote, 16 percent more than was required. As he had tried to think about the possibility that he might not be selected, he also had tried to anticipate the moment and what his reaction would be if the news was good.

What he didn't expect was that his emotions would take over so quickly. The tears began to trickle down his face.

"I had gone over it a thousand times in my mind the way it would come about," Smith said at a news conference later that day. "The only thing I miscalculated was the degree of emotion you get when you do get that phone call. I didn't know how much this was going to touch me. The tears . . . they just come."

Like all great players, Smith didn't begin playing baseball with the goal of making it to the Hall of Fame. He was playing because he enjoyed the game and was good at it, and somewhere along the line, when all of the accolades, like Gold Gloves, were being collected, people began talking about the Hall of Fame.

One of those who was the most vocal in his support of Smith and what his presence meant in the lineup was Whitey Herzog, the man who convinced Smith to accept a trade to the Cardinals from San Diego in the winter of 1981. He told Smith that if he would come play for the Cardinals, they would win a world championship. They did, and two more pennants as well.

"He was so good for the team," Herzog said. "He had a lot of flamboyancy about him, and that got the fans excited. He made all those diving plays—he had a lot of showmanship in him.

"The thing about Ozzie was he never screwed those plays up. He always threw the guy out. He played through a lot of injuries. He also did a great job for me off the field, working and helping the younger players."

Herzog can remember watching Marty Marion play, and Luis Aparicio, and he believes Smith ranks right with them as one of the greatest shortstops in the history of the game.

"If I say he [Ozzie] is the greatest shortstop I've ever seen, I might be lying," Herzog said. "It's hard for me to say that. But I don't see how you can play the position any better than he played it. He didn't have the greatest arm in the world, but even when he hurt the arm, he learned how to still get the job done.

"You could see why the fans loved him, even on the road. You would pay to watch him play just by himself. I was fortunate to have him."

The news that he had been elected to the Hall of Fame, and the warm relationship he still maintains with Herzog, are positives for Smith. As is the case in anyone's life, however, he has had his share of negative moments and disappointments, both in baseball and in his personal life.

His departure as a player in 1996 did not go as he would have liked. He and manager Tony LaRussa were at odds almost from the moment LaRussa arrived in St. Louis, and the relationship was irrevocably broken when Smith was forced into announcing his retirement from the Cardinals.

These days, on the few occasions when he comes to Busch Stadium, it is because of an assignment for CNN-SI or to visit friends on opposing teams. He does not go inside the Cardinals' clubhouse, a place where he does not feel welcome. Even though he received a personal services contract with the Cardinals to continue after his retirement, he has told the organization he will not be involved in any activities as long as LaRussa is the manager.

"I got a chance to meet all the people who worked at the stadium, the security guards, the ticket takers," Smith said. "That's what I miss. Even when we were going bad, they always had kind words. They said, 'It's OK, we'll get them.'"

Smith was a favorite of almost everybody connected with the Cardinals during his stellar career, and he doesn't know why that had to change just because the Cardinals changed managers at the start of the 1996 season.

He had played for Herzog and Joe Torre and had no problems with either manager. There were some who believed that LaRussa felt threatened by Smith, but Smith doesn't know why.

"I don't think he ever gave me a chance," Smith said. "I had been here 18 years and had a pretty good track record. If he had gotten to know me, find out about me, I think it could have been different."

The Cardinals had acquired shortstop Royce Clayton from the Giants during the winter, and going into spring training, LaRussa said there would be an open competition between Smith and Clayton. Whoever had the better spring, he said, would be the starting shortstop.

"I was told I would have a chance to compete to start," Smith said. "If I won the position, it was mine."

Believing he had outplayed Clayton in the spring, Smith was stunned when LaRussa announced that Clayton would be the starting shortstop. Smith believed LaRussa had intended to play Clayton all along and that there never was an open competition for the job.

As Clayton continued to play and Smith rode the bench for the first time in his career, turning down a suggestion that maybe he should move to second base, fans and media began to choose sides, some supporting the manager and others the 13-time Gold Glove shortstop. It was an ugly situation, which finally reached a conclusion in June when Smith announced he would retire at the end of the season.

Smith was honored at each stop as he completed his illustrious career, which came to an official end with the loss to the Atlanta Braves in the National League Championship Series. His last at-bat came as a pinch-hitter in the sixth inning of Game 7, when he popped out.

The tenuous relationship between Smith and LaRussa has not improved since Smith's career ended. Despite some overtures by LaRussa, Smith has made no attempt to reconcile their differences and sees no reason to make an attempt in the near future.

"He had his chance to talk to me man-to-man, to see what I was about when he got here," Smith said. "He considered me a threat. If I was considered a threat then, why would I not be considered a threat now? I don't think it would be good, no. It wasn't a good situation then, why would it have changed?"

At about the same time Smith's professional life was suffering because of his relationship with LaRussa, his personal life was affected as well. His marriage to Denise, whom he met when she was working as an usher at the Astrodome in Smith's rookie season in 1979, ended in divorce.

The couple has three children, and Smith remains a devoted father to sons O.J. and Dustin and daughter Tarya. Cardinals fans who remembered a then four-year-old O.J. running onto the field to copy his dad's trademark back flip for the home opener in 1986 also cheered him at the opening game of the 2002 season, when he sang "God Bless America" after his dad threw out the ceremonial first pitch—with Herzog as his catcher.

In a day filled with emotion, one of the most tender moments occurred when Smith hugged his son as they left the field.

"I've been lucky; I've had a supportive family and loved ones here for me my entire career and my entire life," Smith said.

Part of Smith's extended family includes the legions of Cardinals fans, not only those who pack Busch Stadium each year but those who applaud him while watching the games on television or listening on radio.

They were there cheering the great defensive plays, the back flips that marked special occasions, and—perhaps the most famous moment of Smith's career—the first left-handed homer of his career, which gave the Cardinals a dramatic victory over the Dodgers in Game 5 of the 1985 playoffs.

"Of course, that home run stands out," Smith said of his career. "I remember winning the World Series in 1982, winning the [NL East] pennant in Montreal. Many memories stand out."

He remembers the diving catch in left field, avoiding a collision with incoming outfielder Curt Ford. While a member of the Padres, he made what many consider his greatest fielding play of all time: a bare-handed grab to take a hit away from Jeff Burroughs.

His determination to play through pain was something Smith also remembered.

"I think my greatest achievement was playing from 1985 until 1996 with a torn rotator cuff," Smith said. "You've read or heard I had surgery; I didn't. I just played. I made some adjustments, and I played through the pain."

Smith, who never really spoke of the injury or his diminutive stature during his career, now points out often that he indeed "did have something to prove."

"I was always told I was too small," he said. "I never accepted that. If you pursue excellence, you can achieve it, regardless of your size. There were days when I didn't feel my best, but I made it through."

At the time he accepted Herzog's challenge and approved the trade to the Cardinals, Smith had no idea what his future would be like. Even winning that 1982 World Series did not bring about an accurate forecast of how good his career would turn out to be.

"So much goes into winning a championship. It takes the entire team. That was a real team," Smith said.

Smith's best season offensively came in 1987, his third pennant-winning year in six years. He hit .303 with 75 RBIs. He won yet another Gold Glove in his string of 13, but somehow he was not selected as the league's MVP, finishing second to the last-place Cubs' Andre Dawson.

Maybe Smith's legendary status in St. Louis was best defined during his last All-Star Game at-bat during the 1996 season. He faced Randy Johnson.

Bob Costas, another famous St. Louisan, was announcing the game for NBC.

While seemingly no match for the overpowering "Big Unit," who was then still a member of the Seattle Mariners, Smith turned around on a low fastball and hit it far enough for a home run—but just foul by a matter of feet.

"That would have been sweet," Costas enthusiastically yelled into the microphone as a national audience watched and listened.

Costas let his guard drop and violated the law of the working press box by openly cheering for a player or team. For a moment he wasn't Costas the smooth play-by-play man and sports anchor. He was an Ozzie Smith fan.

Costas is of course not alone in that category. And most of Smith's fans probably don't understand the strained relationship that currently keeps Smith from becoming a more visible part of the Cardinals community, but when they do get a chance to recognize and congratulate him, they do it on every opportunity.

It was his love affair with St. Louis and Cardinals fans that kept Smith from pursuing other opportunities in the major leagues when he retired. He knows he physically could have continued playing, but because of his personal friendships, his business dealings in the community, and his desire to retire as a Cardinal, he turned those opportunities down.

"This is my home. It's special, and I want to be a part of it," Smith said.

While he might not have the presence he once had, or would like to have, in the baseball community, Smith remains very visible and active in the St. Louis business world.

He has operated Ozzie's, one of St. Louis' leading sports bars, since 1987, and he and acclaimed restaurateur David Slay recently opened Smith and Slay's in the affluent suburb of Clayton.

Smith makes dozens of appearances in St. Louis and across the nation on behalf of charitable causes and donates hundreds of hours locally to the Red Cross, Multiple Sclerosis Foundation, Variety Club Telethon, Annie Malone Children's Home, and numerous other causes, continuing a pattern he established during his playing days.

He was awarded the 1995 Roberto Clemente Award for humanitarian and community service and was the 1994 recipient of the Branch Rickey Award. Before Mark McGwire won a St. Louis Man of the Year Award in 1998, Smith became the first athlete to garner the prestigious recognition in 1992.

More recently, Smith was the 2001 recipient of the Walter Payton Sweetness Award. Following the world championship season in 1982, Smith was nominated for the NAACP Image Award for sportsmanship, humanitarian acts, and community involvement.

A tireless representative for St. Louis, Smith has close relationships with several of St. Louis' major corporate CEOs and has worked with the St. Louis Regional Commerce and Growth Association and other civic organizations to extol the virtues of the region for the business community.

Smith has also given financial support to many smaller businesses, including one that was personally costly.

He joined several African-American businesspeople and civic leaders in backing a minority-owned grocery named Sterling's Market in an economically challenged neighborhood on the north side of the city of St. Louis.

Sterling Moody, the store's owner, struggled for months financially before the store closed in late 2001. After Moody was sued by a partner and a judge ruled that a second Moody's store be turned over to that partner, Smith lost an estimated $200,000 investment in the ill-fated grocery store.

Moody sold the store in late 2001 for a reported $400,000.

"Ozzie Smith stepped up to the plate when others would not," said former St. Louis Mayor Freeman R. Bosley Jr., another Moody backer.

Shortly before his retirement, Smith established Ozzie Smith's Sports Academy, and it has grown into one of the nation's best year-round, indoor teaching and training facilities. Smith says the academy's goal "is to maximize the talents of each individual athlete by providing the highest level of quality instruction in a positive training environment."

Smith also has a youth baseball facility in O'Fallon, Missouri, which bears his name. It is one of the finest youth baseball complexes in the region.

Smith has even taken to the stage in St. Louis. He has made appearances in three musicals at the St. Louis Municipal Opera since his retirement, including a starring role in summer 2001 as—fittingly—the Wizard in *The Wizard of Oz*.

"Ozzie was the flamboyant shortstop. He had a flair for drama," said former teammate Bob Forsch.

That natural Ozzie Smith flair had a lot to do with timing, and the Wizard proved it again the night of his Hall of Fame election.

What would the odds be that the Olympic torch would happen to pass through St. Louis that evening?

Smith ran the final St. Louis leg and lit the fire that evening at the downtown Kiener Plaza.

"This is a special night for me. This is a special night for St. Louis," he told a delirious crowd.

Another special moment came on July 28, 2002, when Smith took his place on the stage at the Baseball Hall of Fame in Cooperstown, New York, becoming the 254th player inducted into the shrine.

Not all of St. Louis was there; it just seemed that way. And those who weren't present physically were there in spirit.

Knowing that moment was coming months in advance gave Smith ample opportunity to reflect on his life.

"Growing up in South Central L.A., standing here today as a Hall of Famer, you can't dream this up," Smith said.

16 | John Stuper

It was the fourth inning of a scoreless game. Cornell had loaded the bases with no outs against Yale's freshman right-hander Josh Sowers when head coach John Stuper called time and trotted toward the mound.

Stuper had no doubt been in this position many times during his own playing career, and his years of coaching experience also prepared him for his short conversation with Sowers, who was born seven months after Stuper became the 14th rookie in major league history to be the starting pitcher for two games in the World Series in 1982.

"I told him that I thought their pitcher wasn't that good and I thought we were going to score some runs," Stuper said. "He had to just think an out at a time, and maybe a couple of runs were going to score, but let's keep the damage as light as we can."

The young pitcher nodded his head, but almost before Stuper had sat down in his metal folding chair next to the Yale dugout, the next pitch was headed over the left-field fence for a grand slam.

Sowers and Yale lost the game 5–1, and before the second game of the doubleheader, the pitcher sought out the coach in the dugout for another conversation.

"He asked me to evaluate his performance," Stuper said. "I told him, 'I'm sure there are two pitches you would like to have back, but other than that I thought you did pretty well. You had pretty good location, you had good velocity, you jammed some guys, you were aggressive, all of the things we talk about.' Once in a while you've got to win a game 7–5. If we had scored some runs, their 5 runs wouldn't look so big. He's going to win a lot of games here."

When he was the young pitcher, especially when he was a 25-year-old rookie pitching in a pennant race in St. Louis in 1982, it was Stuper who sought out the advice of older veterans and took their evaluations to heart.

"The second game I pitched in the big leagues was against the Dodgers, and I went five innings and pitched OK," Stuper said. "People were saying, 'Way to battle, Stup,' and I was thinking, 'OK, I pitched pretty good.' We got on the plane to come back to St. Louis, and Jim Kaat sat down next to me. He said, 'How do you think you pitched tonight?' He basically clued me in that I didn't pitch that good. He said, 'You need to do this and you need to do that,' and it really awakened me."

Stuper didn't fully realize it at the time, but he had already begun preparing for his career after his playing days, which ended much sooner than he would have liked or planned. Stuper appeared headed for a long and successful career in the majors during his rookie year, but three years later, his playing days were over.

"He maybe never reached the potential that he should have," Whitey Herzog said. "He was such a nervous kid, a hyper kid."

Stuper was sent back to the minor leagues by the Cardinals in 1984 and was traded to Cincinnati for the 1985 season. He was expecting to stay with the Reds, but they in turn traded him to Montreal before the 1986 season, and when he didn't make the major league team in spring training, he was released.

When his agent could not find another team willing to sign him, Stuper accepted his career change and 20 days later became the baseball coach at his alma mater, Butler County Community College in Pennsylvania.

"I regret that I didn't get to play longer," Stuper said. "Nobody's to blame, and it certainly wasn't a lack of hard work on my part. It just didn't happen; it wasn't meant to be. I thought I could still pitch, but I really think I was a victim of collusion. Montreal wanted to send me to Triple A, but with a much smaller contract; then they could have called me up and saved a lot of money. I didn't want to put all of the work in that would have been required just to get someplace [Montreal] where I didn't want to be.

"I crammed a lot of good things into three years. I got to play for Pete Rose, and I pitched a playoff game and started two games in the World Series and got a ring. I was upset and disappointed, and it took me a couple of years to get over it. I would see a guy pitching on television and say to myself, 'I know I'm better than that guy.' You just have to cope with whatever is thrown your way."

Stuper, who had always assumed his career would end in coaching anyway, went back to school and earned his master's degree in English from Slippery Rock. He left the college ranks in 1989 to begin a two-year stint as a pitching coach in the Cardinals' farm system.

Ever since he began coaching, Stuper had conducted a clinic each winter in Pittsburgh, and a casual conversation he got into one year with the softball coach at Yale led him to apply to become the school's baseball coach. He was selected from a field of 120 applicants and hired in 1993.

"Never did I think I would be the head coach at Yale," said Stuper, now in his 10th year with the Bulldogs, where he ranks as the fourth winningest coach in school history. "Coaching here is kind of a dream job when you think about it, being associated with possibly the greatest university in the world."

Coaching at Yale, in New Haven, Connecticut, presents a different challenge from coaching at a junior college or at a more established collegiate baseball power, such as LSU or Arizona State. Recruiting is more of a challenge, because Stuper has to understand there are some kids, no matter how much he likes them, who aren't going to be coming to school there.

"Our pool isn't as big as everyone else's because of the academic requirements," Stuper said. "You can't fall in love with a kid who gets 950 on the SAT because you're not getting him in. The fringe benefit is the kids you get. Do they make me mad sometimes? Yes, but for the most part they are great kids.

"I was a junior college coach for five years, and my scariest time was between semesters each year to see who was going to be eligible. That's not a concern here. They get their degrees, and they do it in four years. That's just the way it is here."

In his 10 years at Yale, Stuper has had only one player come through his program who did not graduate. That player signed a professional contract after his junior year but is planning on returning to school for two fall semesters to earn his degree, which will give Stuper's program an amazing 100 percent graduation rate.

"Maybe you see us do some stupid things on the field, but these kids are so bright," Stuper said. "There are no physical education or business classes here, no blow-off classes. These guys are all going to be doctors or lawyers or something special.

"I like to say that I'm still the smartest guy on the field, however, because I make out the lineup."

On his current roster, Stuper has players from 14 states, including eight from Florida. Eighty percent of his players receive some kind of financial aid, but Yale gives no athletic scholarships, no merit scholarships, no music scholarships. The university will receive approximately 16,000 applications for admission this year and will accept about 2,000.

"We don't have the pure talent LSU or Arizona State has, but we have smarter kids," Stuper said. "We have kids that maybe aren't the polished product when they get here, so we have to develop them. We've been able to develop some guys here, especially pitchers, and I'm proud of that. We've had 17 players sign professional contracts. If I say a kid can play, scouts will come and see him."

This year's Yale squad has not played as well as Stuper would like, but there are reasons. The team has only three seniors, all pitchers, and has not hit as well as he thought they would. His goal as a manager is one he learned playing for Herzog and Rose—he wants to make his squad as difficult to play against as possible, and that means constantly putting pressure on the opposition by keeping people in motion on offense, getting good pitching, and playing good defense.

"Whitey would tell a guy a couple of innings in advance, 'If this happens and this happens and this happens, you're hitting for Smith,'" Stuper said. "I try to do that too. I picked up more from Whitey and Pete than I thought I did, because I didn't sit there on the bench and say, 'If I'm ever a manager . . .' I want to make our opponents beat us, and I want us to be a pain to play against.

"Whitey was easy to play for; he just said be on time and play hard, and those are my two rules at Yale. I took that from professional baseball. If the bus is leaving at 7:00, that doesn't mean 7:01 or 7:05. It took a little while for these guys to get that. One winter we were having practices at 6:00 A.M. and the bus left the dorm at 5:30. Our catcher missed it, but he ran, with all his equipment, about a mile and a half and got there about one minute late. I gave him some slack because he did put in some effort.

"The best thing to me about coaching at Yale is that I have a kid from Alexander, Arkansas, population 201, and his best friend on the team is from Massachusetts. They would have never crossed paths in their life except for me. Our catcher is from North Carolina, and his best friends are from Queens, Brooklyn, and Long Island. I said, 'What do you guys talk about?' That's really the coolest thing about coaching here."

His former players will never let Stuper forget his first game against traditional rival Harvard. The Bulldogs were 8–0 in the Ivy League, had won 11 in a row, and had just been featured in an article in *USA Today*.

"We were getting our butt kicked, and our shortstop hit a swinging bunt and beat it easily," Stuper said. "The umpire called him out and dressed it up a little bit because there was a pretty good crowd. I was coaching third, and I ran hard to first. My players will tell you I pulled a hamstring, but that didn't happen. The umpire didn't know I was coming, and as he turned around I bumped into him. I was pretty much gone right there, but I argued and got kicked out.

"My boss was there, and since I was kicked out of the game, I had to go stand outside the fence. The Harvard people were having a cookout and party right behind the dugout. They were offering me a Coke and a hot dog. I had steam coming out of my ears, and my boss was there introducing me to the Harvard athletic director and all of these other dignitaries. I'm sure they were thinking, 'If he's your head coach, why is he outside the fence while the game is going on?'

"I don't like to do that, because I think there is something about having Yale across your chest that should keep you from looking like an idiot. There is a certain decorum that goes with wearing a Yale uniform. I also think the way I run a game and the way I coach third is important to my team, and I can't do it from the stands."

In addition to coaching during the season, Stuper runs camps during the summer. Because of the Yale tradition, he often gets the sons and other relatives of famous people at his camps. He has coached the two sons of cartoonist Garry Trudeau and his wife, news anchor Jane Pauley. Last summer the son of television executive Dick Ebersol was in his camp.

"His name was Willie, and he was a great kid," Stuper said. "I asked him, 'You know I don't have a tape of my games from the World Series. Do you think your dad could get it for me?' Just a few days later the tapes showed up at my house."

Even though he has those tapes now, and tapes of some other games he pitched in the major leagues, Stuper will rarely watch them. The only time he watches major league games on a regular basis now is if an outstanding pitcher is working, or during the World Series. He still loves the game but is more focused on what he is doing now than on living in the past.

About the only times he watches himself is when somebody else asks to see the tape. His wife, Pam, whom he married last year, does enjoy watching Stuper in action because she didn't know him at that point in their lives.

Stuper met his future wife, the assistant field hockey coach at Yale, while going through a divorce. He was so out of practice in dating that he had to have a mutual friend ask Pam if she wanted to go out.

"I am so lucky," he said. "She's awesome. She has been all over the world and played in three World Cups for field hockey for the national team. She's gone through a lot of stuff I've gone through in different sports. She is a very accomplished athlete."

She also is a big fan of her husband, and is glad she is able to share happy moments with him now, even if she wasn't around when he was pitching in the World Series in 1982.

Stuper knows there are people who believe his career was shortened because of a sore arm suffered when he continued to pitch the sixth game against the Brewers, going back to the mound after several lengthy rain delays. He admits his arm was sore during that season but denies that he hurt it during the Series game.

"It probably didn't help that I pitched that game," Stuper said. "I got a cortisone shot the next spring, but that was really masking the problem. I found out later when I was traded to Cincinnati the problem was I had a really weak shoulder.

"People think that my greatest memory of 1982 was that game, but it's really not. My most vivid memory is the last out, Bruce Sutter striking out Gorman Thomas and Darrell Porter throwing his mask in the air. That's what stands out. Game 6 is an awesome memory, because I know I was at least a factor in us getting to Game 7. Getting a ring is the prize, because a lot of guys have played a long time and never gotten a ring.

"Back then I don't think I realized how tough it was to do that, or how lucky I was. I realize it now. We had some great veterans who taught me how to be a pro. They were great to me. Doug Bair used to ask me before every start, 'Stup, you scared?' Every start, it was like clockwork. At first it made me mad; then I just laughed. I acted like a rookie, and I minded my p's and q's. I sat next to Kaat on the bench and wondered why every pitcher wasn't doing that. The guy had pitched 25 years in the major leagues—are you kidding me?"

His job now as the coach at Yale also gives Stuper the opportunity to talk baseball with some pretty extraordinary people.

The day the Stupers were closing on their house last fall he got a message on his telephone to call the president of Yale. When he returned the call, the secretary informed him the president had called to find out what time practice was going to be. "Why does he want to know?" Stuper asked. She informed him the team was going to have a special visitor.

The visitor turned out to be the former president of the United States, and former Yale first baseman, George Bush. The first thing he said when he arrived on campus was that he wanted to go to baseball practice. He talked to Stuper for 30 minutes, showing Stuper his knowledge of him and his career by mentioning that he was going to see Stuper's former team, the Cardinals, play at Houston that night.

"He was the nicest guy in the world," Stuper said. "He didn't want to leave. I told him that invariably during the year, when our first baseman misses a pop-up or something, somebody from the stands yells out, 'Bush would have had it.' It was the thrill of a lifetime. Some of these kids are pretty jaded. One of our new freshman's dad is a Secret Service agent who has guarded three presidents. The buzz at practice after he left was something special. It was a big deal even to these Yalies."

On the bookcase in his Yale office is a photo of Bush in his Yale uniform, autographed by the former president with a note to Stuper. He had sent the picture to Stuper after the coach wrote to Bush to wish him happy holidays.

"I wrote the letter, my secretary typed it up, I signed it and [looked at] a copy after I sent it," Stuper said. "As I read the copy of the letter, I noticed in horror that when I thought I had said 'Happy Holidays,' I had really wished the president of the United States and his wife "Happy Hoidays." I had left out the *l*."

Stuper has had feelers from a couple of professional organizations and other colleges about his interest in other jobs, but he is very content at Yale.

"I've got it pretty good here," he said. "I plan to stay as long as they want me.

"My overall goal in life is to someday get on the phone and dial the White House, and when they find out who it is, they put me straight through to the president, because he used to play for me. That's my goal."

17 | Bruce Sutter

One of the things Bruce Sutter used to like the most about being a professional baseball player was the camaraderie of the locker room, hanging out with his friends and buddies, sipping a beer, and talking not only about that day's game but myriad other topics.

It's one of the things he misses the most about not playing baseball anymore, but he has found what he thinks might be one of the closest replacements possible for the locker room—the hunting lodge.

"I have a place up in the mountains in Pennsylvania," Sutter said. "I go up there with my buddies and have a good time. All my sons like to hunt, and so does my brother-in-law. To me the hunting cabin is as close as you can get to the locker room."

Sutter mostly goes deer hunting these days, looking for more trophies to mount and display on the walls of his house, located south and west of Atlanta. Sutter moved to this house, located on 60 mostly wooded acres with a 10-acre lake, when he left the Cardinals and signed with the Braves as a free agent after the 1984 season.

He has hunted all over the United States and Canada for a variety of animals. He has hunted grizzly bear, black bear, elk, and caribou, all of which are displayed at his house.

When he isn't hunting, Sutter often can be found at a baseball game or watching a game on television. His career may have ended prematurely when he injured his arm shortly after signing with the Braves, but that didn't dampen his enthusiasm for the game.

Two of his sons, Chad and Ben, played college baseball. Chad was a catcher at Tulane and was drafted and signed by the Yankees. After one year of pro ball, however, he decided he would rather be a coach and returned to work at Tulane, where he is now the school's pitching coach. His goal is to one day be a college head coach, Sutter said.

His youngest son, Ben, completed his career at Columbus University in Columbus, Georgia, a Division II school, in the spring of 2002. Ben played first base but likely won't be pursuing a professional career. He majored in criminal justice.

Sutter's oldest son, Josh, did not play sports. He is now married and the father of three children, ages 10, 2, and 7 months, making Sutter, who will be 50 in January 2003, a grandfather.

"My beard's a little grayer now," Sutter said, "and I can't throw as hard."

Sutter did spend one year, 1990, working as a pitching coach for the Cardinals' Double A and Triple A farm teams, and although he enjoyed it, he made the decision to quit so he could stay home and watch his sons play. "It was not much of a decision," he said.

Sutter knows his life is about to change, however. With Ben graduating, next year will be the first time since he was seven years old that Sutter won't be spending his summer playing baseball himself or watching his kids play. He still will have plenty of games to watch, however.

Since he moved to Atlanta, Sutter has maintained season tickets for the Braves games in the first row of the stands in left field. He often gives the tickets to his sons, but when he does go, he says, he isn't bothered very often by autograph seekers, mostly because they don't recognize him.

Sutter also has maintained contact with many current major leaguers because of his sons. Corey Patterson, the center fielder for the Cubs, grew up across the street and often works out and takes batting practice in the cage in Sutter's house. He also watched players like Michael Barrett of the Expos and Kris Benson of the Pirates as they were growing up in the Atlanta area.

Chad's best friend is Adam Everett, a shortstop with the Houston Astros and an outstanding prospect.

"I've known those guys since they were 10 or 11 years old," Sutter said. "I've thrown batting practice to them for a long time. Corey and Adam are over here all winter."

Because of his connection with those current players, Sutter doesn't think as often about his own playing career, except when his kids pop in a videotape of one of his games to show their friends.

"They all laugh at me, with my hair blowing, and talk about how skinny I was," Sutter said. "But what an exciting time it was."

And it doesn't seem like 20 years ago that he was pitching in the World Series, until he watches a game on ESPN Classic or a similar channel that features players he competed against over the years.

"The other day they had Len Barker's perfect game on," Sutter said. "Everybody looked different. Their hair was longer, and everybody was a lot skinnier. But the game is still the same."

And it is the game that Sutter still loves, just as much as he did during his playing days.

"I always try to figure out why certain guys are better than other guys and things like that," Sutter said. "I like to think along with them."

One aspect of the game that has changed over the past 20 years is the role of the closer. When Sutter pitched, it wasn't unusual for him to pitch two or sometimes three innings to collect a save. Now closers rarely pitch more than an inning. They are able to collect more saves, but that doesn't mean they are better than Sutter was.

He also was the first pitcher to perfect the split-fingered fastball, which was a key to his success. He refuses to take credit for that, however, or for changing the way the game was played. Sutter says he was just one of several quality closers who came along in his era in the seventies and early eighties, mentioning Goose Gossage, Rollie Fingers, Sparky Lyle, Kent Tekulve, and Tug McGraw.

"Every team had a great relief pitcher back then," Sutter said. "It was different because we didn't use radar guns or stopwatches for everything. We just played the game. I never saw a radar gun until I came to the Cardinals. It didn't matter. We all knew Nolan Ryan threw hard. J. R. Richard threw hard. It didn't matter if it was 95 miles an hour or 100."

Acquiring Sutter to be his closer from the Chicago Cubs was the first move Whitey Herzog knew he had to make if the Cardinals were going to be successful. Herzog knew that with Sutter in his bullpen, his goal each night was to get a 3–2 lead after the seventh inning.

"I knew Bruce would take care of the last two innings," Herzog said. "If we were ahead 3–2 after the seventh inning, I knew we were going to win 9 out of 10 times. There has never been a relief pitcher for seven years who was as good as Sutter. He didn't mind getting you eight outs. Bruce really should be in the Hall of Fame."

Sutter was never better than in the Cardinals' championship season of 1982. He won or saved 45 of the team's 92 victories in the regular season. He had a win and another save in the playoffs against the Braves and another win and two saves in the World Series, including Game 7. His league-leading 36 saves was one short of the National League record at the time, which he set in 1979 while pitching for the Cubs.

He was on the mound for one of the key moments in the regular season, on September 14 in Philadelphia, when the Cardinals were one-half game behind the Phillies for first place in the NL East. The Cardinals were ahead 2–0 in the bottom of the eighth, when the Phillies loaded the bases with one out against John Stuper. Mike Schmidt was coming up to bat.

Herzog summoned Sutter from the bullpen, and Sutter induced Schmidt to hit a comebacker to the mound. Sutter turned it into a 1-2-3 double play and then closed out the win in the ninth. The Cardinals moved ahead of the Phillies into first place and kept the lead for the rest of the season.

Pitching in big games like that was fun for Sutter, but one of the reasons he was able to be so effective was his ability to enjoy the good

Tom Herr was a solid contributor on both offense and defense during the 1982 season.

Image by Lew Portnoy, Spectra-Action Inc.

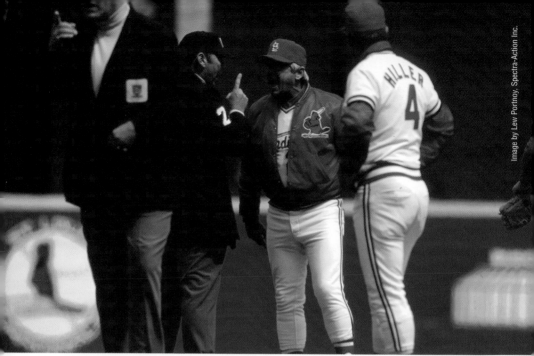

When Whitey Herzog talked, people—even umpires—listened.

Image by Lew Portnoy, Spectra-Action Inc.

Dane Iorg had a great World Series, contributing much to the Cardinals' defeat of the Brewers.

Image by Lew Portnoy, Spectra-Action Inc.

Image by Lew Portnoy, Spectra-Action Inc.

Gene Tenace was one of the key veterans who provided great leadership to the young players of the 1982 club.

Image by Lew Portnoy, Spectra-Action Inc.

When Bruce Sutter was on the mound, the Cardinals were confident that the game would soon be over.

Image by Lew Portnoy, Spectra-Action Inc.

When Ken Oberkfell moved from second base to third, it solidified the Cardinals as having one of the best defensive infields in the game.

Image by Lew Portnoy, Spectra-Action Inc.

Keith Hernandez could always be counted on to come up with a big hit in a clutch situation.

No pitcher was a tougher competitor on the mound than Joaquin Andujar.

Image by Lew Portnoy, Spectra-Action Inc.

Whitey usually didn't have to say too much to Bruce Sutter, who knew what he was in the game to do.

Image by Lew Portnoy, Spectra-Action Inc.

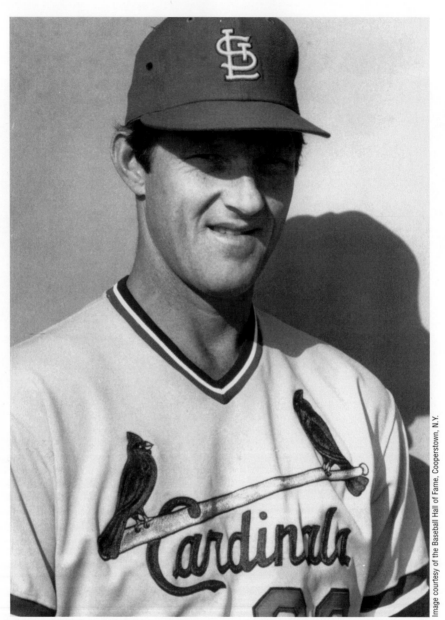

Image courtesy of the Baseball Hall of Fame, Cooperstown, N.Y.

Being able to start or relieve made Jim Kaat a valuable member of the 1982 Cardinals staff.

performances and accept the blame for the bad ones without letting it affect his personality. Seeing him sitting in front of his locker after a game, it was impossible to tell whether he had just struck out the side in the ninth for a save or had given up a game-winning homer to the other team.

As a veteran, he also was a good sounding board for young pitchers on the team, such as Stuper and Dave LaPoint, and he worked well with the other veterans such as Jim Kaat and Gene Tenace in making sure the rookies and other young players did not get out of line.

One of the unanswerable questions about Sutter's career is what would have happened to him, and the Cardinals, had he not left after the 1984 season and signed as a free agent with Atlanta. Would he have hurt his arm had he stayed in St. Louis? Nobody knows or will ever know. Sutter has never lost sleep over that decision or that possibility.

Sutter had hoped to re-sign with the Cardinals but ended up moving to Atlanta when the Cardinals would not agree to include a no-trade clause in his contract. The deal was a financial coup for Sutter—he is still being paid by the Braves through an annuity arrangement—but it was not good for him on the field. He saved only 40 games over three years before an arm injury forced him to retire.

"It's hard, because you know you can't play the way you should," Sutter said. "You still try, but it doesn't matter. You don't want to be embarrassed. You pitch to guys you used to get out fairly easily, and now you're backing up third all the time. That wears on you.

"If I had it to do over again, the one thing I would change is, I had surgery in December, and it was major surgery. They cut me open pretty good. And I was back pitching in spring training. I was never the same after that. That's when I hurt my rotator cuff, because I had not built the strength back up in my arm before I started throwing.

"I guess I was lucky though. I was 33 before my arm blew out, and there are guys in the minors at 19 or 20 who blow out their arm and they're done."

There is no question the greatest times of Sutter's career came in St. Louis, specifically in 1982, when his strikeout of Gorman Thomas brought the Cardinals their first world championship in 15 years.

"It was fun to pitch there," Sutter said. "We had a great defensive club, and we stole a lot of bases, which made the game exciting for the fans. It was a great team, and we knew everything that was going on with everybody. We knew when guys were hurt, and we were there when our kids were born. The guys were all close."

Sutter didn't take up playing golf until he was 35 years old, so in those days he did what many of his teammates did for relaxation—he went fishing early in the morning on lakes in Illinois. He plays more golf than he fishes these days, and he admits that might be a mistake.

"It's hard to be a bad fisherman, but it's easy to be a bad golfer," Sutter said.

Sutter knows that without having his sons' games to watch next summer, he is going to have more free time on his hands to hunt, fish, play golf, or take up some other activity. He thinks it will be similar to adjusting to life after his kids all moved out of the house; it seemed strange at first, but the longer they were gone, the more he grew to like it.

He isn't, however, ruling out a return to a job in baseball in some capacity. He remains good friends with Ted Simmons, the former Cardinal, who now works for the San Diego Padres.

"Ted keeps after me to get back in the game, and I'm still thinking about it," Sutter said. "We'll see what happens."

Appendix I

Newspaper Coverage
of the Cardinals' Championship

Game 1: October 12, 1982
Brewers Trounce Cardinals 10–0 in World Series Opener

It was a discouraging way to start the World Series. In ways they would like to forget, the Cardinals were overwhelmed by the Milwaukee Brewers, 10–0, Tuesday night at Busch Stadium.

They were done in by:

- A pitcher they discarded after looking at him in spring training in 1976.
- Liberal doses of Whiteyball, the type of stuff they have been using to dispose of other teams all season.
- The only real display of the Brewers' well-publicized power, a line-drive homer by Ted Simmons, the popular former Cardinal.

If it is any consolation, the Cardinals also lost the first game of the World Series in 1926, 1931, 1942, 1944, and 1946, all of which they came back to win. They will try again Wednesday night, sending John Stuper against Don Sutton.

For this one, though, it was no contest from the outset. The Brewers scored twice in the first inning against an uncertain and laboring Bob Forsch. It was a long and tedious half inning that took 29 minutes to complete. Both runs were unearned because of an error by Keith Hernandez, but the unearned runs were an omen of things to come.

There was only one solid hit in the inning, but you got the idea early that things would not go well.

They worsened as the Brewers added single runs in the fourth and fifth on a bloop hit by Paul Molitor for the first and the Simmons homer for the second, and then took the game completely out of contention in the sixth when Robin Yount blooped a double for two more runs.

From the start, the crowd of 57,733, which had been so alive and vibrant before the game, had nothing to cheer about. They began drifting out of the chilly weather as early as the seventh inning and Busch Stadium was half empty before the game ended.

There was not a rewarding moment for the Cardinals at any time.

In all, the Brewers had seventeen hits, five by Paul Molitor, the first player in World Series history to produce that many in a single game. Molitor and Robin Yount, who had four, became the 41st and 42nd players in World Series play to have as many as four in a single game. They were also the first to have that many for one team since Joe Garagiola, Whitey Kurowski, and Enos Slaughter each had four for the Red Birds in the fourth game of the 1946 Series in Boston.

On the other side, however, was a superb pitching performance by southpaw Mike Caldwell, a much-traveled 33-year-old who was routed a week ago in the first game of the American League play-offs by California.

In 1976, the Cardinals acquired him from the San Francisco Giants for Willie Crawford and John D'Acquisto, but he never got out of spring training. The Cardinals traded him to the Cincinnati Reds for pitcher Pat Darcy and the Reds subsequently dealt him to Milwaukee for two nonentities.

A 17–13 performer for the Brewers in 1982, Caldwell was devastating mostly because he threw strikes, lots of them.

For seven innings, Caldwell had a one-hitter, a solid double by Darrell Porter in the second inning. Porter added another hit in the eighth and Ken Oberkfell singled later in the frame and that was the extent of the Cardinal attack. All three Cardinal hits were by left-handed batters against a left-handed pitcher.

The only other Cardinal base runner was Tom Herr, who walked with two out in the sixth. In the third, fourth, and fifth, Caldwell's first pitch to every batter was a strike. In all, he threw only 101 pitches, 67 of them strikes.

He had never before won a game at Busch Stadium, being 0–3 while seeing service with the Padres, the Giants, the Pirates, and the Reds.

"It was my best pitching of the year," Caldwell said. "I had good control of my best pitches and with the early lead I was able to make them hit my pitch."

The Cardinals' Whitey Herzog summed it up: "We just took a bad beating. I'm glad we're scheduled for a doubleheader. We were awful. But I've seen Caldwell before and he's a good pitcher."

Herzog said Forsch, who was devastating against Atlanta, had trouble with his control. "He wasn't sharp and his control has to be good. They got some hits on the infield but we've got no excuses."

The long first inning actually settled it. Yount singled to left with one out and Cecil Cooper walked. Forsch's best pitch of the night was a called third strike to Simmons. Forsch seemed out of the inning when Ben Oglivie hit a skidding grounder to Hernandez, but the ball eluded him for an error. Gorman Thomas' single to deep short admitted another and the bases were loaded when Charlie Moore finally fouled out.

A double to left by Moore preceded Molitor's broken bat blooper in the fourth for the third run. Simmons in the fifth inning fouled a pitch deep into the stands in right, and came back with his homer off a column. Yount's pop fly double brought in two more in the sixth.

"It was nice to know that I had so many friends here," said Simmons after the game, acknowledging a big welcome. "I felt a little strange in the third-base dugout."

The Cardinals filed out quietly when it was over. They had little to say. It had been a long night.

—Robert L. Burnes,
St. Louis *Globe-Democrat* executive sports editor

Game 2: October 13, 1982
Cardinals
Bounce Back 5–4

The St. Louis Cardinals won Game 2 of the World Series Wednesday night at Busch Stadium, 5–4, over the Milwaukee Brewers.

They did it the way they've been doing it all year, with unexpected heroes everywhere.

They won it, too, by coming from behind, as they have done so often in 1982, and relying on Bruce Sutter to keep the opposition in check.

Sutter arrived a little earlier than usual, in the seventh inning with the score tied. He worked out of a modest jam and became the winner when the Red Birds squeezed out the winning run in the eighth.

Steve Braun was one of the unexpected heroes. He drew a bases-loaded walk to force in George Hendrick with what proved to be the winning run.

But the big hero, becoming the Cardinals' Mr. October, was catcher Darrell Porter.

In a head to head confrontation with Ted Simmons, his predecessor as Cardinal catcher, Porter emerged the winner even though Simmons homered for the second straight night.

Porter had been outstanding in the National League Championship playoff and was named the most valuable player. And he has picked up the tempo in the Series. Porter had two of the Cards' three hits in the embarrassing 10–0 opening loss Tuesday.

Wednesday he doubled home two runs to tie the score in the sixth inning and then supplied the bridging single in the big eighth inning.

Porter capped off his big evening by snuffing out the last Brewer threat in the ninth. Paul Molitor led off the ninth with a safe bunt. A hit-and-run play failed as Robin Yount swung and missed. Porter's perfect throw to Tommy Herr nailed Molitor trying to steal.

Sutter cut down the last two Milwaukee batters and when Willie McGee squeezed Cecil Cooper's fly ball to end it, the crowd of 53,723, which had been subdued and obviously worried earlier, let out a tremendous roar.

After their embarrassment of Tuesday night, the Cardinals had to fight hard, stave off an early knockout, and then come uphill.

The Cardinals now go to Milwaukee for the next three games. Joaquin Andujar will face Pete Vuckovich Friday night.

Most of all, the hard-earned victory had to restore some of the confidence of the Birds, who had been jolted hard by the first loss.

For half of the game, it appeared that the Brewers had a chance to run away and hide again. They took advantage of control lapses by Stuper. A walk to Gorman Thomas and a double by Charlie Moore produce a run in the second. A single by Paul Molitor, his stolen base, plus a wild pitch, put him in position for an easy score when the Cardinal infield played back and conceded the run as Robin Yount grounded out. Simmons' homer made it 3–0.

Don Sutton, a key figure in the late season and playoffs for the Brewers, was in command in four of the first five innings.

In the third, a single by designated hitter Dane Iorg (one of three DHs Whitey Herzog employed), a force out, and a stolen base by Willie McGee set up Tommy Herr to drive in the first Cardinal run of the Series on a ripping double to right center. He scored a moment later on Ken Oberkfell's single to right.

For the second straight night, the Cardinals' key hitters all season— Keith Hernandez, George Hendrick, and Lonnie Smith—were held hitless. So Herzog and his troops had to work around them.

Milwaukee scored a fourth run in the fifth on a double by Yount—a shot that just missed being a homer—and Cecil Cooper's looping single to left. But the Cards tied in the sixth.

Stuper left after Yount's double. While Jim Kaat gave up the blooper by Cooper, he retired the next two hitters and turned over the job to Doug Bair.

"The relief work of Kaat and Bair in front of Bruce was great," Herzog said. "They kept us in the game. I just wanted to stay close enough to bring in Sutter. It would be awful to go through a World Series without giving Bruce a chance. Heck, I'd miss him."

Sutton began to fade in the sixth. Again Oberkfell was the catalyst with a single to center.

He easily stole the second of three bases the Birds filched off Simmons, and moved to third on Hernandez's fly ball. Hendrick, in the hole with two strikes and no balls, finally enticed a walk.

That set the stage for more Porter heroics. The Brewers overshifted to right field and Porter lofted a Sutton slider into the left-field corner, producing a tie.

"I can't remember the last time I hit one to the left," Porter said afterward. "No, I wasn't trying to do it. But the slider stayed outside and I went with it."

In the eighth, Hernandez walked and was forced by Hendrick. Porter then lashed a single to center. Out went reliever Bob McLure and in came rookie Peter Ladd, who had been devastating in his three appearances out of the bullpen during the American League Championship playoffs.

But his control had deserted him this time. He walked Lonnie Smith to load the bases and then walked Braun to bring in Hendrick with the winning run.

It wasn't gaudy but it was mighty effective, particularly with Engine No. 42 on duty.

Sutter brought the train home on time, with the help of all those heroes. And the Cardinals are alive in the World Series.

—Robert L. Burnes,
St. Louis *Globe-Democrat* executive sports editor

Game 3: October 15, 1982
McGee, Cardinals Bury Brewers in 6–2 Victory

Willie McGee stole Milwaukee's thunder Friday night. The rookie outfielder cracked two homers and pulled off two sensational leaping catches as the Cardinals beat the Brewers at their own game for a 6–2 victory that gave the Red Birds a 2–1 lead in the 79th World Series.

"I don't know of anybody who ever played any better than McGee," Cardinal manager Whitey Herzog said. No other Red Bird performer in the club's proud 56-year history ever accomplished what the 23-year-old freshman displayed before a record County Stadium throng of 56,556.

McGee's incredible effort stunned even him. "I can't believe I'm here," he said.

McGee, obtained in a trade last October with the Yankees for left-handed pitcher Bob Sykes, has been sensational in postseason competition. He homered in the National League playoff sweep against Atlanta and all together knocked in five runs.

The Oakland, California, native broke open the game with a three-run fifth-inning homer against former Cardinal wheelhorse Pete Vuckovich.

Before the American League champion Brewers could mount a challenge, McGee struck again.

Lonnie Smith emerged from his 0-for-7 slump with a triple and double before his outfield sidekick, McGee, bashed Vuckovich for another homer.

The only sour note in the Cardinals' triumph, their second in a row after losing a 10–0 opener at Busch, was an injury to starter/winner Joaquin Andujar.

Andujar, a 15–10 mainstay on the St. Louis staff, had permitted just two hits and was breezing when a smash off Ted Simmons' bat in the seventh knocked him out of the contest.

Simmons' hit forced Andujar out of the contest and before the inning was over, the National League champions again faced a bases-loaded, two-out predicament.

Herzog once again was forced to summon his relief ace, Bruce Sutter, to shut down the majors' number one home-run powerhouse. The Brewers had slugged 216 homers the past season, the Cardinals only 67. If you want to carry it one step further, McGee had connected for only four homers in five months.

Andujar, earning his first Series victory, at least avoided a broken knee. Simmons' wicked hopper struck him just below the right knee and, according to a Mt. Sinai Medical Center spokesman, X-rays were negative.

"He suffered a contusion to the bone and will be able to play if needed," said Larry Tarnoff, vice president of public relations at the hospital.

"If Andujar can't pitch," said a relieved Herzog, looking for a ray of sunshine in the situation, "I'd hope for three or four days of rain."

Both teams went quietly in the first inning, although Cardinal center fielder Willie McGee raced back to the wall for a leaping stab of Brewer Paul Molitor's leadoff smash.

The Cardinals' second produced the first dispute of the Series.

George Hendrick sent a high chopper toward third base that Molitor waited for as third-base umpire Jim Evans called fair. However, St. Louisan Dave Phillips, the umpire stationed at first, thought the ball was foul as Molitor's throw pulled first baseman Cecil Cooper off the bag.

Brewers manager Harvey Kuenn came out to protest the confusion, but Hendrick's first Series hit stood. Porter then grounded to Vuckovich, moving Hendrick to second. Lonnie Smith followed, grounding out to Yount with Hendrick moving to third. Dane Iorg bounced back to Vuckovich to end the threat.

After shortstop Ozzie Smith threw out Roy Howell to begin the Brewers' third, the Brewers put Andujar under the gun when Charlie Moore walked on four pitches. When Andujar put his hand to his mouth, a ball was called with Jim Gantner at bat. Gantner then doubled to right, sending Moore to third.

Andujar, however, struck out Molitor on a 3–2 sidearm pitch and Yount rolled meekly to second baseman Tom Herr and the threat vanished.

After Porter was called out on strikes in the fifth, a decision he argued, Lonnie Smith got his first hit of the Series, a double to left on which he fell rounding first base.

Cooper mishandled Iorg's grounder to Cooper's right for an error and McGee jumped on Vuckovich's first pitch for a drive into the right-field bleachers to give the Cards a 3–0 lead. One of the runs was unearned.

The Cardinals pulled away in the seventh when Lonnie Smith plugged the gap in right-center field for a triple and came on to score when Gantner's relay went into the Cardinal dugout for an error.

After Iorg flied to Thomas, McGee smacked a 1–0 pitch about 25 feet inside the right-field foul pole for his second homer of the game and a 5–0 lead.

With one out in the Milwaukee seventh, Simmons cracked a one-bounce hopper that hit Andujar just below his right knee. The St. Louis pitcher went down and rolled over in agony as the ball rolled toward the third-base line for a hit.

Dr. Stan London, team surgeon, and trainer Gene Gieselmann rushed out to look at Andujar. The Cardinal hurler was carried off the field and was described in stable condition before being taken to Mt. Sinai Medical Center for X-rays.

Jim Kaat replaced Andujar and struck out Ben Oglivie before Gorman Thomas singled to left. Doug Bair was brought on to pitch after Don Money had been announced as a pinch-hitter for designated hitter Roy Howell. Money then walked, loading the bases. Sutter came in, the third pitcher in the inning, and threw one pitch, which Moore lifted for a foul pop that third baseman Ken Oberkfell grabbed, leaning into the Cardinal dugout for a fine play.

—Jack Herman,
St. Louis *Globe-Democrat* sportswriter

Game 4: October 16, 1982
Under October's Microscope, Little Things Mean a Lot

The World Series is baseball under a microscope. In 162 games, the little things tend to even out.

In seven games, the littlest things can kill you.

In 162 games, it's permissible, inevitable, to give one away now and then. And not suffer in the end.

In just seven, if you give one away, you must win five times to be the World Champions.

Saturday, the Cardinals did just that. They made this a five-of-seven challenge for themselves by kicking away a game against the Brewers that would have all but locked up the 1982 Series.

It was reminiscent of 1968. Game 5 at Detroit. Lou Brock didn't slide at the plate. The Tigers battled back to win and then took two more in St. Louis to retrieve a Series that appeared irrevocably lost.

In Game 4 here Saturday, the Cards had shelled Moose Haas from the mound and were one clean catch and seven outs away from a comfortable victory.

It was becoming boring. The game and the Series. With a 5–1 lead in the seventh inning, a 3–1 advantage in games was at the Red Birds' fingertips.

That was when Dave LaPoint took Keith Hernandez's toss just above the pocket of his glove, dropped it for an error, and an easy inning was transformed into a nightmare.

A nightmare under a microscope.

Instead of two outs, nobody on, instead of seven simple outs to get, the Brewers had been presented an opportunity that they magnified into six runs and a 2–2 Series deadlock.

LaPoint's error on the ground ball off Ben Oglivie's bat to Hernandez was the littlest thing that made the most difference Saturday, but it wasn't the only small aspect that sabotaged the Cardinals.

Robin Yount attempted to check his swing with two outs, bases loaded, and the Cards still seemingly safe at 5–2.

Another little thing: the ball arched into right field for two runs. Then Cecil Cooper sliced one just past Ken Oberkfell. . . .

Well, you know the rest. A lot of little things added up to the Brewer's 7–5 victory—keeping the Red Birds two games short of the four they need for this championship, instead of one.

What's a single game? What's one victory? In 162 games, it's nothing. In seven, it's a magnified opportunity wasted.

But World Series baseball is linkage under the microscope, too.

It wasn't just LaPoint's error. It went beyond the sequence of Yount's checked swing and Gorman Thomas' deciding two-run single.

It actually went back to Friday night, to Joaquin Andujar's injury, to his exit from Game 3.

If . . .

If Ted Simmons had not disposed of Andujar with his shot off the Card pitcher's right leg, Andujar was a good bet to finish his mound artistry against the Brewers.

He was working on a three-hit shutout. He was ahead, 5–0. He is known for finishing what he starts.

But when he departed, Whitey Herzog tried to seal the victory first with Jim Kaat and then with Doug Bair. Unsatisfactorily.

So Bruce Sutter had to be summoned to get seven outs, to face 10 batters.

If Andujar had finished Friday, Sutter would have been available Saturday afternoon. But because of Andujar's injury, Sutter couldn't play Horatio for the besieged Red Birds in that nightmare seventh inning.

Another little thing in a long season. A monumental one in a short series.

Then there is the case of Rollie Fingers, the Brewers' neutralizer for Sutter out of the bullpen.

Milwaukee's pitching here on Saturday was Bob McClure, who came on in the eighth to face Wallbanger Willie McGee with two on and one out.

McClure is a left-hander. McGee is a better left-handed hitter than right. But if Fingers was available, what would Harvey Kuenn have done in that situation?

You go with your best, right? Even if he is right-handed.

McClure turned McGee around, put him two steps further from first base—and got him into a bang-bang double play to end the inning.

And in the ninth, McClure also turned around Ozzie Smith and Tommy Herr and sent Oberkfell (the Cards' third most-productive batter to that point in the Series) to the bench so another right-hander, Gene Tenace, could bat. He retired all three easily.

Just a week previously, in St. Louis, all the little things worked in the Cardinals' favor as they beat the Braves 5–4 at Busch to go up 2–0 in their National League playoff.

Who won that game in the ninth? Obie, of course, with a liner over the center fielder's head after a walk and a sacrifice.

Why was Obie hitting against the Braves? Because Joe Torre didn't have a left-handed pitcher on his staff.

The Braves won their division without a left-hander, but that was over 162 games. They could work around that deficiency over the long haul.

But in a short series, everything is magnified. One error. One checked swing. One unavailable relief pitcher. Another out of the bullpen to take advantage of baseball's precious percentages.

And, of course, one other thing becomes magnified under October's microscope: a ballgame is lost that appeared won.

It's a large assignment to have to win five out of seven in the World Series.

—Rich Koster,
St. Louis *Globe-Democrat* sportswriter

Game 5: October 17, 1982
Brewers Push Cardinals to Wall

They all came to praise Milwaukee's Robin Yount, a virtual shoo-in for the American League's Most Valuable Player Award and a likely MVP in the 79th World Series, as he sparked the Brewers to a 6–4 victory Sunday.

The quiet shortstop of the Brewers, with a record-breaking 4-for-4 batting performance, hit one double, two singles, and a homer off starter/loser Bob Forsch to help push the Cardinals into a 3–2 corner in the Series.

His homer came with two away in the seventh for what seemed a commanding 4–2 lead. The Brewers then reached Cardinal ace reliever Bruce Sutter in the eighth for their final two runs, which proved to be the difference in Game 5.

The Cardinals kept coming on, however, and finished with fifteen hits, including four in the ninth inning that brought the potential winning run to the plate in pinch-hitter Gene Tenace.

Tenace, batting for Ken Oberkfell, who had three hits, flied out to end the game. The game was seen by 56,562 patrons, breaking the attendance record at Milwaukee County Stadium.

"I knew Obie had three hits," Cardinal manager Whitey Herzog said, "but I wanted to take a crack at a home run and I thought Tenace could do it."

By then, one-time Cardinal castoff pitcher Mike Caldwell had been excused, after yielding 14 hits. Fellow left-hander Bob McClure, who had saved Saturday's 7–5 triumph for Milwaukee, allowed a run-scoring single to George Hendrick before striking out Willie McGee. McClure then induced Tenace to fly out to left fielder Ben Oglivie.

As a result, the Brewers now hold a three-to-two lead in the best-of-seven fall classic. Yount is 11-for-21 and the only player in Series history to collect four hits apiece in two games.

The second Forsch-Caldwell match-up of this Series bore no resemblance to the first. In the opener at Busch Stadium, Caldwell fired a three-hitter at the National League champions.

This time, it seemed that the Red Birds had him on the ropes a number of times.

"After [lead-off batsman] Lonnie Smith hit that line drive back at me," Caldwell said, I knew it wasn't going to be easy. I knew they'd try to adjust after seeing me the first time and try to hit the ball up the middle and into the holes. They waited on me more this time."

Caldwell characterized the game, in which he struck out three and walked two while throwing 128 pitches, as a "typical basic Caldwell game, eight or nine hits. I don't try to overpower anybody. You've got to give them credit. Keith Hernandez hit the ball well today and George hit me up the middle. Oberkfell did a super job, too."

Smith singled off Caldwell's glove in the first inning and stole second as David Green struck out. With a 2–0 count on Hernandez, Smith tried to steal third with a headfirst slide and was nailed by catcher Ted Simmons' throw to third baseman Paul Molitor.

"If you make that play, it's a good one," Herzog said. "If you don't, it's a bad play. The book says you can steal third on Caldwell. We just didn't get it done."

Hernandez, 0-for-15 in the Series, maintained he wasn't concerned about his lack of production and quickly reversed his Series batting performance.

After Lonnie Smith was cut down at third, Hernandez singled to right for his first of three hits. Oberkfell and Hendrick also fashioned three-hit efforts, but the Cardinals undermined their offense by stranding 12 runners.

The Brewers got the jump on the Cardinals in the bottom of the first inning on Yount's hit off Forsch's leg and Cecil Cooper's single, which advanced Yount to second. While pitching to Simmons, Forsch wheeled and tried to pick off Yount at second and threw into center field for an error.

The runners advanced, and Yount scored on Simmons' groundout to Hernandez.

The Cardinals scored the equalizer the hard way in the third when Green drilled a triple past charging right fielder Charlie Moore and came across on Hernandez's double to left center. Gorman Thomas narrowly missed a diving try on Hernandez's smash.

The Brewers retaliated in their half when Forsch walked Molitor, who reached third on Yount's double to left.

Cooper grounded to Hernandez, who was prepared for a possible play at the plate until the ball bad-hopped at the last instant, and he flipped to Forsch for the putout at first base. Molitor scored on the play.

The A.L. sluggers continued to receive maximum mileage out of their economical offense with a fifth-inning double by Moore and Molitor's single to left. Yount also singled to Oberkfell's back hand, but Forsch escaped a bases-loaded mess by striking out old friend Simmons.

The Cardinals, putting at least a runner aboard in every round, crept within 3–2 in their seventh. Ozzie Smith coaxed a walk from Caldwell and held at second when Lonnie Smith singled to right.

Green flied out and Hernandez hit a shot to first baseman Cooper, who got a force-out at second, Ozzie reaching third. Caldwell, accepting the relay at first, went down, but the Cardinal shortstop said the Milwaukee pitcher was up in ho hurry and he had no chance to score.

Hendrick, with his 33rd birthday coming up Monday, singled to center to score Ozzie.

With two away in the home half of the seventh, the right-handed-hitting Yount drilled a fastball into the right-field bleachers.

The 27-year-old Yount, who once considered golf as a career, said, "Yes, I'm definitely convinced baseball is my game."

"Yount is a great player, an all-around player," said Herzog, who remembers him from his tour as an A.L. manager at Texas and Kansas City. "I'd have to say he ranks among the top three in baseball. Nobody can play any better. We kept trying to get the ball in a spot and every time we got it in that spot, he hit it."

The fact that the Brewers tapped Sutter for three eighth-inning hits and two big runs did not concern Herzog.

"He's just a human being," Herzog said. "He's not going to get you out every time. The thing that hurt him was the walk. With a good-hitting team like the Brewers, the walk will hurt you."

Sutter earned a save here Friday night and a victory in Game 2 at St. Louis, when the Cardinals literally walked to a 5–4 triumph.

Hernandez cited Milwaukee's defense as the "key." His club, he said, got a "bunch of hits—on the nose—but right at people. It's one of those things."

The Cardinals, down by four runs in the ninth, might have given the Brewers something to think about when the Series returns to St. Louis Tuesday night.

After Molitor deprived Lonnie Smith of a third hit to start the ninth, Green doubled to left and Hernandez followed with his second double, making it 6–3. Hendrick's run-scoring single—he and Hernandez accounted for all four St. Louis RBIs—finished Caldwell. Darrell Porter ripped McClure's first pitch for another hit, but the Cardinals had reached the end of the line.

Moore recalled that he and Yount had joined the Brewers at the same time. "It's a pleasure to have watched him grow as a person and player each year. He's put everything together this year, and he's smarter and stronger."

Forsch did not enter a dissenting vote, except to say that, "if I had the strike zone Yount had, I could hit .300, too. I'm not taking anything away from him, but I know certain pitches I made on him were strikes and were not called.

"I think we showed our character in the ninth by battling back. We've won two in a row before."

Simmons, having spent 11 seasons with the Cardinals, said there will not be an advantage for either team in the return to downtown St. Louis.

"These are two teams trying to beat each other's brains out," he said.

—Jack Herman,
St. Louis *Globe-Democrat* sportswriter

Game 6: October 19, 1982
Cards' Bats Boom
as Thunder Rolls

The Cardinals trampled the Milwaukee Brewers and fought off the wind and the rain to win the sixth game of the World Series Tuesday night, 13–1, at Busch Stadium and set up a seventh and final game Wednesday night.

Joaquin Andujar, the Cardinals' wounded warrior ace, will work for the Birds in the finale against Pete Vuckovich of the Brewers. In the third game Andujar and the Cardinals won, 5–2, over Vuke.

Beating the Brewers on Tuesday night was far more easily accomplished than beating the weather.

Rookie John Stuper pitched superbly, limiting the Brewers to two singles through six innings when the game was halted a second time. At that point he had retired 11 men in a row and, with the help of two double plays, had faced only one over the minimum at that point.

He yielded a run in the ninth inning, spoiling his chance to become the first rookie since 1948 to pitch a World Series shutout.

He was aided by a boisterous assault on veteran Don Sutton, a late season hero for the Brewers who has not won a game at Busch Stadium since 1976.

They pounded out 10 hits through the first six innings, including king-sized home runs by Darrell Porter and Keith Hernandez and two doubles and a triple by designated hitter Dane Iorg. Iorg became the first DH in history to collect three extra base hits in a World Series game. Additionally, Iorg had a slugging percentage of 1.000—13 bases in 13 times at bat.

Even though Commissioner Bowie Kuhn insisted that the game would be played to its normal conclusion—"We are prepared to wait many hours," he said—the Brewers gave every evidence of being ready to retire. After the first rain delay, they brought in Doc Medich without warm-up as a second reliever.

Sal Bando of the Brewers said while manager Harvey Kuenn "was not conceding this game, he wanted to save regulars for a seventh game, plus the fact that some of the players could stiffen up during the delay."

The Cardinals jumped on Sutton early. Iorg hit a double into the left-field corner, where Ben Oglivie had to fight off two walls, got a hand on the ball, but couldn't hold it.

Sutton seemed out of the inning when Willie McGee rolled to shortstop Robin Yount, the star of the Series so far, but the ball rolled by him for an error to score Iorg. Tom Herr, demoted to eighth in the batting order because of a woeful Series slump, lashed a drive into the right-field corner. McGee never hesitated and, urged on by coach Chuck Hiller, scored easily when Ted Simmons couldn't handle the throw.

Lonnie Smith tried to steal home in the third, almost made it and, in the opinion of many, did make it. He had reached first on Jim Gantner's error and stolen second with a belly-flop slide during which he injured his ring finger. He moved to third on Hernandez's groundout.

As Sutton faced George Hendrick, Smith measured the pitcher once, then took off for home. Umpire Jim Evans of the American League called him out but the television replay indicated rather clearly that Smith was in under the throw.

"I had a perfect view of the play," said umpire Evans. "In my judgment, Simmons tagged his hand before it touched the plate."

The home runs widened the lead and took the game out of contention. Porter smashed one in the fourth after Hendrick singled. Iorg went into his act again, this time a triple to right, and came home on Herr's perfectly executed squeeze bunt. In the fifth Lonnie Smith blooped a hit to right and came home when Hernandez unloaded his homer into the runway in right center.

There had been a slight drizzle in the second inning, thunder and lightning in the third. As the Cardinals batted in the fourth, the rain came down more heavily. As the Brewers came to bat in the fifth, three outs were needed to make it an official game.

Stuper continued steadily and each out drew a roar from the crowd. When the inning was over and the game was now in the hands of the elements, the umpires, and the commissioner, the crowd let out a roar that matched anything the Milwaukee crowds had done.

A second rain delay halted play with the Cards at bat in the sixth, a run in, and two on. It would last more than two hours.

"This is the best game I've ever pitched," Stuper said. "This is a dream come true for me."

For Don Sutton, in his fourth World Series (the other three with the Dodgers) but so far never on a winner, it was summed up like this: "I had good stuff, poor location, and several poorly executed good ideas. Against a good-hitting club, that adds up to defeat."

What happened after play resumed at 11:40 was academic and was contested for about half as many fans as were there earlier—but the two-hour, 15-minute wait didn't still the Cardinal bats.

David Green walked to load the bases following resumption. Ken Oberkfell forced McGee at the plate but Hernandez singled and it added up to a six-run inning.

The Cardinals were not certain about Stuper's arm and they had Jim Kaat warming in case the rookie could not make it.

But Stuper was obviously pumped up, intent only on throwing strikes. He retired the side in order in the seventh and a wide throw by Oberkfell provided a base runner for Milwaukee in the eighth—but that was the only threat the Brewers could muster that inning.

Stuper's rookie shutout—the last was by Gene Bearden of Cleveland in 1948—went by the boards on Gantner's double, Paul Molitor's single, and a wild pitch.

That made the final score 13–1 and that may be significant. In 1968, the Cardinals went into the sixth game of the Series leading Detroit, three games to two. But the Tigers came back to win the last two—the only time the Cardinals have ever lost a seven-game series.

The score of that sixth game? 13–1.

—Robert L. Burnes,
St. Louis *Globe-Democrat* executive sports editor

Game 7: October 20, 1982

World Champs!

All the Cardinals heroes came thundering home in the final game of the World Series. Almost methodically, they did what they had been doing all year as they whipped the Milwaukee Brewers 6–3 in a pulsating, exciting climax.

The Cardinals surrendered the lead momentarily in the top of the sixth inning. Then Ozzie and Lonnie Smith, the catalysts all year, sparked the rally that regained the lead.

With that as a start, the climax guys, Keith Hernandez and George Hendrick, delivered the tying and go-ahead runs.

Joaquin Andujar, although not at his best after taking a shot in the leg in the third game off the bat of Ted Simmons, gamely battled his way through seven innings. His own error had been instrumental in the one big surge the Brewers had when they moved ahead in the sixth inning.

He maneuvered through the seventh inning as Bruce Sutter limbered up in the bullpen.

Sutter took over in the eighth and that's all she wrote for the Brewers. He cut down six straight Brewers through the heart of their lineup, fanning Gorman Thomas to end the game.

The moment it ended, the Cardinals dashed on the field to congratulate Sutter for doing his thing, but also to congratulate each other on a job well done—for 162 games and through the seven matches of the World Series.

A good portion of the crowd of 53,723 dashed on the field as the game ended, despite stern warnings over the public-address system, despite the presence of mounted police.

The field became a sea of red, matching the fireworks that exploded over Busch Stadium.

The celebration went on for 40 minutes; then the horses urged the fans off the field.

For the Cardinals it was their ninth world championship, the most by any National League team. It was the seventh time in eight tries that they won a Series that went to the final game.

The victory came as the Cardinals won so many games all year.

"That's the way we did it," said manager Whitey Herzog, delighted with his first world championship after three frustrations with division winners in Kansas City.

"Joaquin pitched with a lot of guts and Bruce finished it up. It was typical."

Andujar admitted that his bruised leg bothered him, but said, "I never lost confidence in myself or in the other guys. I wanted to win. So did they."

In the early innings, the Cardinals squandered opportunities against Pete Vuckovich. They left eight runners stranded in the first four innings.

They negotiated one run in the fourth on singles by Willie McGee, Tom Herr, and Lonnie Smith.

But the Brewers, using the weapon they used all season, tied the score in the fifth inning with one swing of the bat—a home run by Ben Oglivie, his first RBI of the Series.

Then the Brewers took a page from the Cardinal book of "Whiteyball" to move ahead in the sixth inning.

The pesky Jim Gantner, the Brewers' steadiest hitter, led off the sixth with a double. Paul Molitor bunted, as he had done safely 10 times during the season, and when Andujar threw off balance, the ball went wild, Gantner scored, and Molitor reached second. Robin Yount, who had the MVP locked up until the last two games, beat out an infield hit and Cecil Cooper hit a sacrifice fly. The Brewers led by a pair, 3–1.

But only for a moment.

Ozzie and Lonnie went into their act, singling and doubling successively to left.

Milwaukee manager Harvey Kuenn pulled the struggling Vuckovich in favor of lefty Bob McClure, who had been troublesome to the Cardinals earlier. Herzog removed Ken Oberkfell for Gene Tenace, a maneuver he had tried twice before without success against McClure. This time Tenace enticed a walk to load the bases for Keith Hernandez.

The Cardinal first baseman, on his 29th birthday, came through handsomely with a single to right field, sending home the tying runs as the crowd went wild. Hernandez, after a slow start, came on strong in the last three games.

Hendrick then punched a single to right, sending home Mike Ramsey—running for Tenace—with the go-ahead run, to make it 4–3.

"That not only was the winning hit," Herzog said afterward, "but it demonstrated why George is so great. They've been pitching him outside all through the Series. This time he went to right field with the pitch. Great work."

That was the game, but the Cardinals broke the Brewers' heart with two more runs in the eighth inning.

The runs served two purposes. They made Sutter's job a little easier; they also made certain that Darrell Porter would be the Most Valuable Player in the Series.

Lonnie Smith—that man again—opened the eighth inning. Ramsey fanned as the Brewers, in desperation, brought in two-game winner Mike Caldwell. Hernandez was walked deliberately and Hendrick flied out. But Porter lashed a single to right field for a big run and Steve Braun, the third designated hitter employed by the Cards, duplicated.

For Porter, it was a great end to the season. He had hitting problems during the season and was constantly compared to Simmons, the man he replaced.

Despite two early homers by Simmons, who was no hitting factor in the late going, Porter was clearly the superior in the Series.

All the Cardinal heroes had a part, playing Whitey Herzog's game right down to the finish. It was a great night for Cardinal president Gussie Busch, who started the final drive by riding onto the field for the third time on the Anheuser-Busch wagon pulled by the Clydesdale eight-horse hitch. Gussie wanted this one. It was a dream come true for him.

"The greatest night of my life," he said.

Maybe Ozzie Smith typified the whole thing.

As he went into position at the start of the game, the Wizard of Oz did a back flip at second base. As Sutter fanned Thomas, Ozzie did it again.

The Cardinals had turned the baseball world upside down, thanks to Ozzie and Lonnie and Keith and George and Willie and, of course, Bruce Sutter.

—Robert L. Burnes,
St. Louis *Globe-Democrat* executive sports editor

Appendix II

Statistical Tables: Pitchers

Table Key

W   wins

L   losses

Pct. winning percentage

G   games

GS   games started

CG   complete games

SHO shutouts

SV   saves

IP   innings pitched

H   hits

BB   walks

SO   strikeouts

ERA earned run average

Joaquin Andujar

Year	Team	W	L	Pct.	G	GS	CG	SHO	SV	IP	H	BB	SO	ERA
1976	HOU NL	9	10	.474	28	25	9	4	0	172.1	163	75	59	3.60
1977	HOU NL	11	8	.579	26	25	4	1	0	158.2	149	64	69	3.69
1978	HOU NL	5	7	.417	35	13	2	0	1	110.2	88	58	55	3.42
1979	HOU NL	12	12	.500	46	23	8	0	4	194.0	168	88	77	3.43
1980	HOU NL	3	8	.273	35	14	0	0	2	122.0	132	43	75	3.91
1981	HOU NL	2	3	.400	9	3	0	0	0	23.2	29	12	18	4.94
	STL NL	6	1	.857	11	8	1	0	0	55.1	56	11	19	3.74
	TOTAL	8	4	.667	20	11	1	0	0	79.0	85	23	37	4.10
1982	STL NL	15	10	.600	38	37	9	5	0	265.2	237	50	137	2.47
1983	STL NL	6	16	.273	39	34	5	2	1	225.0	215	75	125	4.16
1984	STL NL	20	14	.588	36	36	12	4	0	261.1	218	70	147	3.34
1985	STL NL	21	12	.636	38	38	10	2	0	269.2	265	82	112	3.40
1986	OAK AL	12	7	.632	28	26	7	1	1	155.1	139	56	72	3.82
1987	OAK AL	3	5	.375	13	13	1	0	0	60.2	63	26	32	6.08
1988	HOU NL	2	5	.286	23	10	0	0	0	78.2	94	21	35	4.00
13 Yrs.		127	118	.518	405	305	68	19	9	2153.0	2016	731	1032	3.58

Doug Bair

Year	Team	W	L	Pct.	G	GS	CG	SHO	SV	IP	H	BB	SO	ERA
1976	PIT NL	0	0	—	4	0	0	0	0	6.1	4	5	4	5.68
1977	OAK AL	4	6	.400	45	0	0	0	8	83.1	78	57	68	3.46
1978	CIN NL	7	6	.538	70	0	0	0	28	100.1	87	38	91	1.97
1979	CIN NL	11	7	.611	65	0	0	0	16	94.1	93	51	86	4.29
1980	CIN NL	3	6	.333	61	0	0	0	6	85.0	91	39	62	4.24
1981	CIN NL	2	2	.500	24	0	0	0	0	39.0	42	17	16	5.77
	STL NL	2	0	1.000	11	0	0	0	1	15.2	13	2	14	3.45
	TOTAL	4	2	.667	35	0	0	0	1	54.2	55	19	30	5.10
1982	STL NL	5	3	.625	63	0	0	0	8	91.2	69	36	68	2.55
1983	STL NL	1	1	.500	26	0	0	0	1	29.2	24	13	21	3.03
	DET AL	7	3	.700	27	1	0	0	4	55.2	51	19	39	3.88
	TOTAL	8	4	.667	53	1	0	0	5	85.1	75	32	60	3.58
1984	DET AL	5	3	.625	47	1	0	0	4	93.2	82	36	57	3.75
1985	DET AL	2	0	1.000	21	3	0	0	0	49.0	54	25	30	6.24
	STL NL	0	0	—	2	0	0	0	0	2.0	1	2	0	0.00
	TOTAL	2	0	1.000	23	3	0	0	0	51.0	55	27	30	5.99
1986	OAK AL	2	3	.400	31	0	0	0	4	45.0	37	18	40	3.00
1987	PHI NL	2	0	1.000	11	0	0	0	0	13.2	17	5	10	5.93
1988	TOR AL	0	0	—	10	0	0	0	0	13.1	14	3	8	4.05
1989	PIT NL	2	3	.400	44	0	0	0	1	67.1	52	28	56	2.27
1990	PIT NL	0	0	—	22	0	0	0	0	24.1	30	11	19	4.81
15	Yrs.	55	43	.561	584	5	0	0	81	909.1	839	405	689	3.63

Bob Forsch

Year	Team	W	L	Pct.	G	GS	CG	SHO	SV	IP	H	BB	SO	ERA
1974	STL NL	7	4	.636	19	14	5	2	0	100.0	84	34	39	2.97
1975	STL NL	15	10	.600	34	34	7	4	0	230.0	213	70	108	2.86
1976	STL NL	8	10	.444	33	32	2	0	0	194.0	209	71	76	3.94
1977	STL NL	20	7	.741	35	35	8	2	0	217.1	21	69	95	3.48
1978	STL NL	11	17	.393	34	34	7	3	0	233.2	205	97	114	3.70
1979	STL NL	11	11	.500	33	32	7	1	0	218.2	215	52	92	3.83
1980	STL NL	11	10	.524	31	31	8	0	0	214.2	225	33	87	3.77
1981	STL NL	10	5	.667	20	20	1	0	0	124.1	106	29	41	3.18
1982	STL NL	15	9	.625	36	34	6	2	1	233.0	238	54	69	3.48
1983	STL NL	10	12	.455	34	30	6	2	0	187.0	190	54	56	4.28
1984	STL NL	2	5	.286	16	11	1	0	0	52.1	64	19	21	6.02
1985	STL NL	9	6	.600	34	19	3	1	2	136.0	132	47	48	3.90
1986	STL NL	14	10	.583	33	33	3	0	0	230.0	211	68	104	3.25
1987	STL NL	11	7	.611	33	30	2	1	0	179.0	189	45	89	4.32
1988	STL NL	9	4	.692	30	12	1	1	0	108.2	111	38	40	3.73
	HOU NL	1	4	.200	6	6	0	0	0	27.2	42	6	14	6.51
	TOTAL	10	8	.556	36	18	1	1	0	136.1	153	44	54	4.28
1989	HOU NL	4	5	.444	37	15	0	0	0	108.1	133	46	40	5.32
16 Yrs.		**168**	**136**	**.55**	**498**	**422**	**67**	**19**	**3**	**2794.2**	**2777**	**832**	**1133**	**3.76**

Jim Kaat

Year	Team	W	L	Pct.	G	GS	CG	SHO	SV	IP	H	BB	SO	ERA
1959	WAS AL	0	2	.000	3	2	0	0	0	5.0	7	4	2	12.60
1960	WAS AL	1	5	.167	13	9	0	0	0	50.0	48	31	25	5.58
1961	MIN AL	9	17	.346	36	29	8	1	0	200.2	188	82	122	3.90
1962	MIN AL	18	14	.563	39	35	16	5	1	269.0	243	75	173	3.14
1963	MIN AL	10	10	.500	31	27	7	1	1	178.1	195	38	105	4.19
1964	MIN AL	17	11	.607	36	34	13	0	1	243.0	231	60	171	3.22
1965	MIN AL	18	11	.621	45	42	7	2	2	264.1	267	63	154	2.83
1966	MIN AL	25	13	.658	41	41	19	3	0	304.2	271	55	205	2.75
1967	MIN AL	16	13	.552	42	38	13	2	0	263.1	269	42	211	3.04
1968	MIN AL	14	12	.538	30	29	9	2	0	208.0	192	40	130	2.94
1969	MIN AL	14	13	.519	40	32	10	0	1	242.1	252	75	139	3.49
1970	MIN AL	14	10	.583	45	34	4	1	0	230.1	244	58	120	3.56
1971	MIN AL	13	14	.481	39	38	15	4	0	260.1	275	47	137	3.32
1972	MIN AL	10	2	.833	15	15	5	0	0	113.1	94	20	64	2.06
1973	MIN AL	11	12	.478	29	28	7	2	0	181.2	206	39	93	4.41
	CHI AL	4	1	.800	7	7	3	1	0	42.2	44	4	16	4.22
	TOTAL	15	13	.536	36	35	10	3	0	224.1	250	43	109	4.37
1974	CHI AL	21	13	.618	42	39	15	3	0	277.1	263	63	142	2.92
1975	CHI AL	20	14	.588	43	41	12	1	0	303.2	321	77	142	3.11
1976	PHI NL	12	14	.462	38	35	7	1	0	227.2	241	32	83	3.48
1977	PHI NL	6	11	.353	35	27	2	0	0	160.1	211	40	55	5.39
1978	PHI NL	8	5	.615	26	24	2	1	0	140.1	150	32	48	4.10
1979	PHI NL	1	0	1.000	3	1	0	0	0	8.1	9	5	2	4.32
	NY AL	2	3	.400	40	1	0	0	2	58.1	64	14	23	3.86
	TOTAL	3	3	.500	43	2	0	0	2	66.2	73	19	25	3.91
1980	NY AL	0	1	.000	4	0	0	0	0	5.0	8	4	1	7.20
	STL NL	8	7	.533	49	14	6	1	4	129.2	140	33	36	3.82
	TOTAL	8	8	.500	53	14	6	1	4	134.2	148	37	37	3.94
1981	STL NL	6	6	.500	41	1	0	0	4	53.0	60	17	8	3.40
1982	STL NL	5	3	.625	62	2	0	0	2	75.0	79	23	35	4.08
1983	STL NL	0	0	—	24	0	0	0	0	34.2	48	10	19	3.89
25 Yrs.		283	237	.544	898	625	180	31	18	4530.1	4620	1083	2461	3.45

Jeff Keener*

Year	Team	W	L	Pct.	G	GS	CG	SHO	SV	IP	H	BB	SO	ERA
1982	STL NL	1	1	.500	19	0	0	0	0	22.1	19	19	25	1.61
1983	STL NL	0	0	—	4	0	0	0	0	4.1	6	1	4	8.31
2 Yrs.		**1**	**1**	**.500**	**23**	**0**	**0**	**0**	**0**	**26.2**	**25**	**20**	**29**	**2.70**

*No batting statistics are listed for Jeff Keener because he never batted in the majors.

Jeff Lahti

Year	Team	W	L	Pct.	G	GS	CG	SHO	SV	IP	H	BB	SO	ERA
1982	STL NL	5	4	.556	33	1	0	0	0	56.2	53	21	22	3.81
1983	STL NL	3	3	.500	53	0	0	0	0	74.0	64	29	26	3.16
1984	STL NL	4	2	.667	63	0	0	0	1	84.2	69	34	45	3.72
1985	STL NL	5	2	.714	52	0	0	0	19	68.1	63	26	41	1.84
1986	STL NL	0	0	—	4	0	0	0	0	2.1	3	1	3	0.00
5 Yrs.		17	11	.607	205	1	0	0	20	286.0	252	111	137	3.12

Dave LaPoint

Year	Team	W	L	Pct.	G	GS	CG	SHO	SV	IP	H	BB	SO	ERA
1980	MIL AL	1	0	1.000	5	3	0	0	1	15.0	17	13	5	6.00
1981	STL NL	1	0	1.000	3	2	0	0	0	10.7	12	2	4	4.22
1982	STL NL	9	3	.750	42	21	0	0	0	152.7	170	52	81	3.42
1983	STL NL	12	9	.571	37	29	1	0	0	191.3	191	84	113	3.95
1984	STL NL	12	10	.545	33	33	2	1	0	193.0	205	77	130	3.96
1985	SF NL	7	17	.292	31	31	2	1	0	206.7	215	74	122	3.57
1986	DET AL	3	6	.333	16	8	0	0	0	67.7	85	32	36	5.72
	SD NL	1	4	.200	24	4	0	0	0	61.3	67	24	41	4.26
	TOTAL	4	10	.286	40	12	0	0	0	129.0	152	56	77	5.02
1987	STL NL	1	1	.500	6	2	0	0	0	16.0	26	5	8	6.75
	CHI AL	6	3	.667	14	12	2	1	0	82.7	69	31	43	2.94
	TOTAL	7	4	.636	20	14	2	1	0	98.7	95	36	51	3.55
1988	CHI AL	10	11	.476	25	25	1	1	0	161.3	151	47	79	3.40
	PIT NL	4	2	.667	8	8	1	0	0	52.0	54	10	19	2.77
	TOTAL	14	13	.519	33	33	2	1	0	213.3	205	57	98	3.24
1989	NY AL	6	9	.400	20	20	0	0	0	113.7	146	45	51	5.62
1990	NY AL	7	10	.412	28	27	2	0	0	157.7	180	57	67	4.11
1991	PHI NL	0	1	.000	2	2	0	0	0	5.0	10	6	3	16.20
12 Yrs.		80	86	.482	294	227	11	4	1	1486.7	1598	559	802	4.02

Mark Littell

Year	Team	W	L	Pct.	G	GS	CG	SHO	SV	IP	H	BB	SO	ERA
1973	KC AL	1	3	.250	8	7	1	0	0	38.0	44	23	16	5.68
1975	KC AL	1	2	.333	7	3	1	0	0	24.1	19	15	19	3.70
1976	KC AL	8	4	.667	60	1	0	0	16	104.0	68	60	92	2.08
1977	KC AL	8	4	.667	48	5	0	0	12	104.2	73	55	106	3.61
1978	STL NL	4	8	.333	72	2	0	0	11	106.1	80	59	130	2.79
1979	STL NL	9	4	.692	63	0	0	0	13	82.1	60	39	67	2.19
1980	STL NL	0	2	.000	14	0	0	0	2	10.2	14	7	7	9.28
1981	STL NL	1	3	.250	28	1	0	0	2	41.0	36	31	22	4.39
1982	STL NL	0	1	.000	16	0	0	0	0	20.2	22	15	7	5.23
9 Yrs.		**32**	**31**	**.508**	**316**	**19**	**2**	**0**	**56**	**532.0**	**416**	**304**	**466**	**3.32**

John Martin

Year	Team	W	L	Pct.	G	GS	CG	SHO	SV	IP	H	BB	SO	ERA
1980	STL NL	2	3	.400	9	5	1	0	0	42.0	39	9	23	4.29
1981	STL NL	8	5	.615	17	15	4	0	0	102.2	85	26	36	3.42
1982	STL NL	4	5	.444	24	7	0	0	0	66.0	56	30	21	4.23
1983	STL NL	3	1	.750	26	5	0	0	0	66.1	60	26	29	3.53
	DET AL	0	0	—	15	0	0	0	1	13.1	15	4	11	7.43
	TOTAL	3	1	.750	41	5	0	0	1	79.2	75	30	40	4.18
4 Yrs.		17	14	.548	91	32	5	0	1	290.2	255	95	120	3.94

Steve Mura

Year	Team	W	L	Pct.	G	GS	CG	SHO	SV	IP	H	BB	SO	ERA
1978	SD NL	0	2	.000	5	2	0	0	0	7.2	15	5	5	11.74
1979	SD NL	4	4	.500	38	5	0	0	2	73.0	57	37	59	3.08
1980	SD NL	8	7	.533	37	23	3	1	2	168.2	149	86	109	3.68
1981	SD NL	5	14	.263	23	22	2	0	0	138.2	156	50	70	4.28
1982	STL NL	12	11	.522	35	30	7	1	0	184.1	196	80	84	4.05
1983	CHI AL	0	0	—	6	0	0	0	0	12.1	13	6	4	4.38
1985	OAK AL	1	1	.500	23	1	0	0	1	48.0	41	25	29	4.13
7 Yrs.		**30**	**39**	**.435**	**167**	**83**	**12**	**2**	**5**	**632.2**	**627**	**289**	**360**	**4.00**

Eric Rasmussen

Year	Team	W	L	Pct.	G	GS	CG	SHO	SV	IP	H	BB	SO	ERA
1975	STL NL	5	5	.500	14	13	2	1	0	81.0	86	20	59	3.78
1976	STL NL	6	12	.333	43	17	2	1	0	150.3	139	54	76	3.53
1977	STL NL	11	17	.393	34	34	11	3	0	233.0	223	63	120	3.48
1978	STL NL	2	5	.286	10	10	2	1	0	60.3	61	20	32	4.18
	SD NL	12	10	.545	27	24	3	2	0	146.3	154	43	59	4.06
	TOTAL	14	15	.483	37	34	5	3	0	206.7	215	63	91	4.09
1979	SD NL	6	9	.400	45	20	5	3	3	156.7	142	42	54	3.27
1980	SD NL	4	11	.267	40	14	0	0	1	111.3	130	33	50	4.37
1982	STL NL	1	2	.333	8	3	0	0	0	18.3	21	8	15	4.42
1983	STL NL	0	0	—	6	0	0	0	1	7.7	16	4	6	11.74
	KC AL	3	6	.333	11	9	2	1	0	52.7	61	22	18	4.78
	TOTAL	3	6	.333	17	9	2	1	1	60.3	77	26	24	5.66
8 Yrs.		**50**	**77**	**.394**	**238**	**144**	**27**	**12**	**5**	**1017.7**	**1033**	**309**	**489**	**3.85**

Andy Rincon

Year	Team	W	L	Pct.	G	GS	CG	SHO	SV	IP	H	BB	SO	ERA
1980	STL NL	3	1	.750	4	4	1	0	0	31.0	23	7	22	2.61
1981	STL NL	3	1	.750	5	5	1	1	0	35.7	27	5	13	1.77
1982	STL NL	2	3	.400	11	6	1	0	0	40.0	35	25	11	4.72
3 Yrs.		**8**	**5**	**.615**	**20**	**15**	**3**	**1**	**0**	**106.7**	**85**	**37**	**46**	**3.12**

John Stuper

Year	Team	W	L	Pct.	G	GS	CG	SHO	SV	IP	H	BB	SO	ERA
1982	STL NL	9	7	.563	23	21	2	0	0	136.2	137	55	53	3.36
1983	STL NL	12	11	.522	40	30	6	1	1	198.0	202	71	81	3.68
1984	STL NL	3	5	.375	15	12	0	0	0	61.1	73	20	19	5.28
1985	CIN NL	8	5	.615	33	13	1	0	0	99.0	116	37	38	4.55
4 Yrs.		**32**	**28**	**.533**	**111**	**76**	**9**	**1**	**1**	**495.0**	**528**	**183**	**191**	**3.96**

Bruce Sutter

Year	Team	W	L	Pct.	G	GS	CG	SHO	SV	IP	H	BB	SO	ERA
1976	CHI NL	6	3	.667	52	0	0	0	10	83.1	63	26	73	2.70
1977	CHI NL	7	3	.700	62	0	0	0	31	107.1	69	23	129	1.34
1978	CHI NL	8	10	.444	64	0	0	0	27	99.0	82	34	106	3.18
1979	CHI NL	6	6	.500	62	0	0	0	37	101.1	67	32	110	2.22
1980	CHI NL	5	8	.385	60	0	0	0	28	102.1	90	34	76	2.64
1981	STL NL	3	5	.375	48	0	0	0	25	82.1	64	24	57	2.62
1982	STL NL	9	8	.529	70	0	0	0	36	102.1	88	34	61	2.90
1983	STL NL	9	10	.474	60	0	0	0	21	89.1	90	30	64	4.23
1984	STL NL	5	7	.417	71	0	0	0	45	122.2	109	23	77	1.54
1985	ATL NL	7	7	.500	58	0	0	0	23	88.1	91	29	52	4.48
1986	ATL NL	2	0	1.000	16	0	0	0	3	18.2	17	9	16	4.34
1988	ATL NL	1	4	.200	38	0	0	0	14	45.1	49	11	40	4.76
12 Yrs.		**68**	**71**	**.489**	**661**	**0**	**0**	**0**	**300**	**1042.0**	**879**	**309**	**861**	**2.83**

Appendix III

Statistical Tables: Hitters

Table Key

G   games

AB   at-bats

R   runs

H   hits

2B   doubles

3B   triples

HR   home runs

RBI runs batted in

SB   stolen bases

BB   bases on balls

SO   strikeouts

BA   batting average

OBP on-base percentage

SLG slugging percentage

TB   total bases

Joaquin Andujar*

Year	Team	G	AB	R	H	2B	3B	HR	RBI	SB	BB	SO	BA	OBP	SLG	TB
1976	HOU NL	28	57	4	8	1	0	0	1	0	2	29	.140	.169	.158	9
1977	HOU NL	26	53	6	10	2	0	0	2	0	3	27	.189	.232	.226	12
1978	HOU NL	36	23	0	3	1	0	0	3	0	1	11	.130	.167	.174	4
1979	HOU NL	46	57	3	5	1	0	2	7	0	2	32	.088	.117	.211	12
1980	HOU NL	35	29	3	5	0	1	1	3	0	3	16	.172	.250	.345	10
1981	HOU NL	9	4	0	0	0	0	0	0	0	1	3	.000	.200	.000	0
	STL NL	12	19	0	0	0	0	0	0	0	0	9	.000	.000	.000	0
	TOTAL	21	23	0	0	0	0	0	0	0	1	12	.000	.042	.000	0
1982	STL NL	38	95	3	15	1	1	0	4	1	0	44	.158	.158	.189	18
1983	STL NL	39	73	2	6	1	0	0	2	2	2	38	.082	.107	.096	7
1984	STL NL	36	84	8	11	1	0	2	8	1	9	47	.131	.215	.214	1
1985	STL NL	38	94	2	10	2	0	0	8	3	5	50	.106	.152	.128	12
1988	HOU NL	23	19	0	4	2	0	0	0	0	2	9	.211	.286	.316	6
13 Yrs.		**407**	**607**	**31**	**77**	**12**	**2**	**5**	**38**	**7**	**30**	**315**	**.127**	**.168**	**.178**	**108**

* Andujar had no at-bats in 1986 and 1987.

Doug Bair*

Year	Team	G	AB	R	H	2B	3B	HR	RBI	SB	BB	SO	BA	OBP	SLG	TB
1978	CIN NL	70	14	1	2	0	0	0	1	0	0	4	.143	.143	.143	2
1979	CIN NL	65	8	0	0	0	0	0	0	0	0	5	.000	.000	.000	0
1980	CIN NL	61	2	0	0	0	0	0	0	0	0	1	.000	.000	.000	0
1981	CIN NL	24	3	1	1	0	0	1	3	0	0	1	.333	.333	1.333	4
	STL NL	11	3	0	0	0	0	0	0	0	0	3	.000	.000	.000	0
	TOTAL	35	6	1	1	0	0	1	3	0	0	4	.167	.167	.667	4
1982	STL NL	63	13	0	1	0	0	0	0	0	0	3	.077	.077	.077	1
1983	STL NL	26	2	0	0	0	0	0	0	0	0	2	.000	.000	.000	0
	DET AL	27	0	0	0	0	0	0	0	0	0	0	—	—	—	0
	TOTAL	53	2	0	0	0	0	0	0	0	0	2	.000	.000	.000	0
1987	PHI NL	11	1	0	0	0	0	0	0	0	0	0	.000	.000	.000	0
1989	PIT NL	44	5	0	1	1	0	0	0	0	0	3	.200	.200	.400	2
1990	PIT NL	22	1	0	0	0	0	0	0	0	0	1	.000	.000	.000	0
15 Yrs.		**584**	**52**	**2**	**5**	**1**	**0**	**1**	**4**	**0**	**0**	**23**	**.096**	**.096**	**.173**	**9**

* Bair had no at-bats 1976–1977, 1984–1986, and 1988.

Steve Braun

Year	Team	G	AB	R	H	2B	3B	HR	RBI	SB	BB	SO	BA	OBP	SLG	TB
1971	MIN AL	128	343	51	87	12	2	5	35	8	48	50	.254	.350	.344	118
1972	MIN AL	121	402	40	116	21	0	2	50	4	45	38	.289	.360	.356	143
1973	MIN AL	115	361	46	102	28	5	6	42	4	74	48	.283	.408	.438	158
1974	MIN AL	129	453	53	127	12	1	8	40	4	56	51	.280	.361	.364	165
1975	MIN AL	136	453	70	137	18	3	11	45	0	66	55	.302	.389	.428	194
1976	MIN AL	122	417	73	120	12	3	3	61	12	67	43	.288	.384	.353	147
1977	SEA AL	139	451	51	106	19	1	5	31	8	80	59	.235	.351	.315	142
1978	SEA AL	32	74	11	17	4	0	3	15	1	9	5	.230	.310	.405	30
	KC AL	64	137	16	36	10	1	0	14	3	28	16	.263	.386	.350	48
	TOTAL	96	211	27	53	14	1	3	29	4	37	21	.251	.360	.370	78
1979	KC AL	58	116	15	31	2	0	4	10	0	22	11	.267	.384	.388	45
1980	KC AL	14	23	0	1	0	0	0	1	0	2	2	.043	.120	.043	1
	TOR AL	37	55	4	15	2	0	1	9	0	8	5	.273	.365	.364	20
	TOTAL	51	78	4	16	2	0	1	10	0	10	7	.205	.295	.269	21
1981	STL NL	44	46	9	9	2	1	0	2	1	15	7	.196	.393	.283	13
1982	STL NL	58	62	6	17	4	0	0	4	0	11	10	.274	.384	.339	21
1983	STL NL	78	92	8	25	2	1	3	7	0	21	7	.272	.404	.413	38
1984	STL NL	86	98	6	27	3	1	0	16	0	17	17	.276	.383	.327	32
1985	STL NL	64	67	7	16	4	0	1	6	0	10	9	.239	.342	.343	23
15 Yrs.		**1425**	**3650**	**466**	**989**	**155**	**19**	**52**	**388**	**45**	**579**	**433**	**.271**	**.371**	**.367**	**1338**

Glenn Brummer

Year	Team	G	AB	R	H	2B	3B	HR	RBI	SB	BB	SO	BA	OBP	SLG	TB
1981	STL NL	21	30	2	6	1	0	0	2	0	1	2	.200	.219	.233	7
1982	STL NL	35	64	4	15	4	0	0	8	2	0	12	.234	.234	.297	19
1983	STL NL	45	87	7	24	7	0	0	9	1	10	11	.276	.351	.356	31
1984	STL NL	28	58	3	12	0	0	1	3	0	3	7	.207	.246	.259	15
1985	TEX AL	49	108	7	30	4	0	0	5	1	11	22	.278	.355	.315	34
5 Yrs.		**178**	**347**	**23**	**87**	**16**	**0**	**1**	**27**	**4**	**25**	**54**	**.251**	**.304**	**.305**	**106**

Bob Forsch

Year	Team	G	AB	R	H	2B	3B	HR	RBI	SB	BB	SO	BA	OBP	SLG	TB
1974	STL NL	20	29	1	7	1	0	0	1	1	2	11	.241	.290	.276	8
1975	STL NL	35	78	9	24	3	3	1	5	0	3	20	.308	.341	.462	36
1976	STL NL	35	62	6	11	2	0	1	5	0	1	17	.177	.190	.258	16
1977	STL NL	35	72	6	12	4	0	0	4	0	2	29	.167	.189	.222	16
1978	STL NL	34	83	2	15	7	0	1	8	0	1	26	.181	.190	.301	25
1979	STL NL	33	73	7	8	2	2	0	5	0	5	17	.110	.162	.192	14
1980	STL NL	32	78	11	23	5	0	3	10	1	2	18	.295	.312	.474	37
1981	STL NL	20	41	0	5	1	0	0	3	0	1	10	.122	.143	.146	6
1982	STL NL	36	73	7	15	3	1	0	3	0	3	20	.205	.237	.274	20
1983	STL NL	37	54	4	13	3	0	1	6	0	3	14	.241	.271	.352	19
1984	STL NL	16	16	1	4	1	0	0	3	0	0	3	.250	.250	.312	5
1985	STL NL	34	45	3	11	2	1	1	4	0	0	10	.244	.244	.400	18
1986	STL NL	34	76	7	13	4	1	2	12	0	0	24	.171	.169	.329	25
1987	STL NL	34	57	9	17	6	0	2	8	0	3	17	.298	.333	.509	29
1988	STL NL	31	25	3	7	0	0	0	2	1	1	6	.280	.308	.280	7
	HOU NL	6	7	0	1	1	0	0	3	0	0	1	.143	.143	.286	2
	TOTAL	37	32	3	8	1	0	0	5	1	1	7	.250	.273	.281	9
1989	HOU NL	37	24	1	4	0	0	0	2	0	0	6	.167	.167	.167	4
16 Yrs.		**509**	**893**	**77**	**190**	**45**	**8**	**12**	**84**	**3**	**27**	**249**	**.213**	**.235**	**.321**	**287**

Julio Gonzalez

Year	Team	G	AB	R	H	2B	3B	HR	RBI	SB	BB	SO	BA	OBP	SLG	TB
1977	HOU NL	110	383	34	94	18	3	1	27	3	19	45	.245	.287	.316	121
1978	HOU NL	78	223	24	52	3	1	1	16	6	8	31	.233	.263	.269	60
1979	HOU NL	68	181	16	45	5	2	0	10	2	5	14	.249	.280	.298	54
1980	HOU NL	40	52	5	6	1	0	0	1	1	1	8	.115	.132	.135	7
1981	STL NL	20	22	2	7	1	0	1	3	0	1	3	.318	.348	.500	11
1982	STL NL	42	87	9	21	3	2	1	7	1	1	24	.241	.258	.356	31
1983	DET AL	12	21	0	3	1	0	0	2	0	1	7	.143	.182	.190	4
7 Yrs.		**370**	**969**	**90**	**228**	**32**	**8**	**4**	**66**	**13**	**36**	**132**	**.235**	**.269**	**.297**	**288**

David Green

Year	Team	G	AB	R	H	2B	3B	HR	RBI	SB	BB	SO	BA	OBP	SLG	TB
1981	STL NL	21	34	6	5	1	0	0	2	0	6	5	.147	.275	.176	6
1982	STL NL	76	166	21	47	7	1	2	23	11	8	29	.283	.315	.373	62
1983	STL NL	146	422	52	120	14	10	8	69	34	26	76	.284	.325	.422	178
1984	STL NL	126	452	49	121	14	4	15	65	17	20	105	.268	.297	.416	188
1985	SF NL	106	294	36	73	10	2	5	20	6	22	58	.248	.301	.347	102
1987	STL NL	14	30	4	8	2	1	1	1	0	2	5	.267	.312	.500	15
6 Yrs.		489	1398	168	374	48	18	31	180	68	84	278	.268	.308	.394	551

George Hendrick

Year	Team	G	AB	R	H	2B	3B	HR	RBI	SB	BB	SO	BA	OBP	SLG	TB
1971	OAK AL	42	114	8	27	4	1	0	8	0	3	20	.237	.254	.289	33
1972	OAK AL	58	121	10	22	1	1	4	15	3	3	22	.182	.205	.306	37
1973	CLE AL	113	440	64	118	18	0	21	61	7	25	71	.268	.308	.452	199
1974	CLE AL	139	495	65	138	23	1	19	67	6	33	73	.279	.322	.444	220
1975	CLE AL	145	561	82	145	21	2	24	86	6	40	78	.258	.304	.431	242
1976	CLE AL	149	551	72	146	20	3	25	81	4	51	82	.265	.323	.448	247
1977	SD NL	152	541	75	168	25	2	23	81	11	61	74	.311	.381	.492	266
1978	SD NL	36	111	9	27	4	0	3	8	1	12	16	.243	.317	.360	40
	STL NL	102	382	55	110	27	1	17	67	1	28	44	.288	.337	.497	190
	TOTAL	138	493	64	137	31	1	20	75	2	40	60	.278	.332	.467	230
1979	STL NL	140	493	67	148	27	1	16	75	2	49	62	.300	.359	.456	225
1980	STL NL	150	572	73	173	33	2	25	109	6	32	67	.302	.342	.498	285
1981	STL NL	101	394	67	112	19	3	18	61	4	41	44	.284	.356	.485	191
1982	STL NL	136	515	65	145	20	5	19	104	3	37	80	.282	.323	.450	232
1983	STL NL	144	529	73	168	33	3	18	97	3	51	76	.318	.373	.493	261
1984	STL NL	120	441	57	122	28	1	9	69	0	32	75	.277	.324	.406	179
1985	CAL AL	16	41	5	5	1	0	2	6	0	4	8	.122	.196	.293	12
	PIT NL	69	256	23	59	15	0	2	25	1	18	42	.230	.278	.312	80
	TOTAL	85	297	28	64	16	0	4	31	1	22	50	.215	.266	.310	92
1986	CAL AL	102	283	45	77	13	1	14	47	1	26	41	.272	.332	.473	134
1987	CAL AL	65	162	14	39	10	0	5	25	0	14	18	.241	.301	.395	64
1988	CAL AL	69	127	12	31	1	0	3	19	0	7	20	.244	.283	.323	41
18 Yrs.		**2048**	**7129**	**941**	**1980**	**343**	**27**	**267**	**1111**	**59**	**567**	**1013**	**.278**	**.329**	**.446**	**3178**

Keith Hernandez

Year	Team	G	AB	R	H	2B	3B	HR	RBI	SB	BB	SO	BA	OBP	SLG	TB
1974	STL NL	14	34	3	10	1	2	0	2	0	7	8	.294	.415	.441	15
1975	STL NL	64	188	20	47	8	2	3	20	0	17	26	.250	.309	.362	68
1976	STL NL	129	374	54	108	21	5	7	46	4	49	53	.289	.376	.428	160
1977	STL NL	161	560	90	163	41	4	15	91	7	79	88	.291	.379	.459	257
1978	STL NL	159	542	90	138	32	4	11	64	13	82	68	.255	.351	.389	211
1979	STL NL	161	610	116	210	48	11	11	105	11	80	78	.344	.417	.513	313
1980	STL NL	159	595	111	191	39	8	16	99	14	86	73	.321	.408	.494	294
1981	STL NL	103	376	65	115	27	4	8	48	12	61	45	.306	.401	.463	174
1982	STL NL	160	579	79	173	33	6	7	94	19	100	67	.299	.397	.413	239
1983	STL NL	55	218	34	62	15	4	3	26	1	24	30	.284	.352	.431	94
	NY NL	95	320	43	98	8	3	9	37	8	64	42	.306	.424	.434	139
	TOTAL	150	538	77	160	23	7	12	63	9	88	72	.297	.396	.433	233
1984	NY NL	154	550	83	171	31	0	15	94	2	97	89	.311	.409	.449	247
1985	NY NL	158	593	87	183	34	4	10	91	3	77	59	.309	.384	.430	255
1986	NY NL	149	551	94	171	34	1	13	83	2	94	69	.310	.413	.446	246
1987	NY NL	154	587	87	170	28	2	18	89	0	81	104	.290	.377	.436	256
1988	NY NL	95	348	43	96	16	0	11	55	2	31	57	.276	.333	.417	145
1989	NY NL	75	215	18	50	8	0	4	19	0	27	39	.233	.324	.326	70
1990	CLE AL	43	130	7	26	2	0	1	8	0	14	17	.200	.283	.238	31
17 Yrs.		2088	7370	1124	2182	426	60	162	1071	98	1070	1012	.296	.384	.436	3214

Tom Herr

Year	Team	G	AB	R	H	2B	3B	HR	RBI	SB	BB	SO	BA	OBP	SLG	TB
1979	STL NL	14	10	4	2	0	0	0	1	1	2	2	.200	.333	.200	2
1980	STL NL	76	222	29	55	12	5	0	15	9	16	21	.248	.299	.347	77
1981	STL NL	103	411	50	110	14	9	0	46	23	39	30	.268	.329	.345	142
1982	STL NL	135	493	83	131	19	4	0	36	25	57	56	.266	.341	.320	158
1983	STL NL	89	313	43	101	14	4	2	31	6	43	27	.323	.403	.412	129
1984	STL NL	145	558	67	154	23	2	4	49	13	49	56	.276	.335	.346	193
1985	STL NL	159	596	97	180	38	3	8	110	31	80	55	.302	.379	.416	248
1986	STL NL	152	559	48	141	30	4	2	61	22	73	75	.252	.342	.331	185
1987	STL NL	141	510	73	134	29	0	2	83	19	68	62	.263	.346	.331	169
1988	STL NL	15	50	4	13	0	0	1	3	3	11	4	.260	.393	.320	16
	MIN AL	86	304	42	80	16	0	1	21	10	40	47	.263	.349	.326	99
	TOTAL	101	354	46	93	16	0	2	24	13	51	51	.263	.356	.325	115
1989	PHI NL	151	561	65	161	25	6	2	37	10	54	63	.287	.352	.364	204
1990	PHI NL	119	447	39	118	21	3	4	50	7	36	47	.264	.320	.351	157
	NY NL	27	100	9	25	5	0	1	10	0	14	11	.250	.342	.330	33
	TOTAL	146	547	48	143	26	3	5	60	7	50	58	.261	.324	.347	190
1991	NY NL	70	155	17	30	7	0	1	14	7	32	21	.194	.328	.258	40
	SF NL	32	60	6	15	1	1	0	7	2	13	7	.250	.384	.300	18
	TOTAL	102	215	23	45	8	1	1	21	9	45	28	.209	.344	.270	58
13 Yrs.		**1514**	**5349**	**676**	**1450**	**254**	**41**	**28**	**574**	**188**	**627**	**584**	**.271**	**.347**	**.350**	**1870**

Dane Iorg

Year	Team	G	AB	R	H	2B	3B	HR	RBI	SB	BB	SO	BA	OBP	SLG	TB
1977	PHI NL	12	30	3	5	1	0	0	2	0	1	3	.167	.194	.200	6
	STL NL	30	32	2	10	1	0	0	4	0	5	4	.312	.395	.344	11
	TOTAL	42	62	5	15	2	0	0	6	0	6	7	.242	.304	.274	17
1978	STL NL	35	85	6	23	4	1	0	4	0	4	10	.271	.300	.341	29
1979	STL NL	79	179	12	52	11	1	1	21	1	12	28	.291	.337	.380	68
1980	STL NL	105	251	33	76	23	1	3	36	1	20	34	.303	.349	.438	110
1981	STL NL	75	217	23	71	11	2	2	39	2	7	9	.327	.344	.424	92
1982	STL NL	102	238	17	70	14	1	0	34	0	23	23	.294	.352	.361	86
1983	STL NL	58	116	6	31	9	1	0	11	1	10	11	.267	.321	.362	42
1984	STL NL	15	28	3	4	2	0	0	3	0	2	6	.143	.200	.214	6
	KC AL	78	235	27	60	16	2	5	30	0	13	15	.255	.287	.404	95
	TOTAL	93	263	30	64	18	2	5	33	0	15	21	.243	.278	.384	101
1985	KC AL	64	130	7	29	9	1	1	21	0	8	16	.223	.268	.331	43
1986	SD NL	90	106	10	24	2	1	2	11	0	2	21	.226	.239	.321	34
10 Yrs.		**743**	**1647**	**149**	**455**	**103**	**11**	**14**	**216**	**5**	**107**	**180**	**.276**	**.317**	**.378**	**622**

Jim Kaat*

Year	Team	G	AB	R	H	2B	3B	HR	RBI	BB	SO	BA	OBP	SLG	TB
1959	WAS AL	3	1	0	0	0	0	0	0	0	1	.000	.000	.000	0
1960	WAS AL	13	14	0	2	0	0	0	0	0	6	.143	.143	.143	2
1961	MIN AL	47	63	10	15	3	1	0	1	4	13	.238	.294	.317	20
1962	MIN AL	48	100	9	18	3	1	1	10	8	40	.180	.239	.260	26
1963	MIN AL	36	61	2	8	1	0	1	8	2	19	.131	.185	.197	12
1964	MIN AL	46	83	11	14	1	0	3	11	11	31	.169	.263	.289	24
1965	MIN AL	56	93	6	23	4	0	1	9	3	29	.247	.265	.323	30
1966	MIN AL	47	118	12	23	2	1	2	13	5	41	.195	.228	.280	33
1967	MIN AL	45	99	7	17	3	1	1	4	7	26	.172	.226	.253	25
1968	MIN AL	36	77	7	12	3	0	0	5	2	18	.156	.177	.195	15
1969	MIN AL	43	87	8	18	8	0	2	10	4	20	.207	.247	.368	32
1970	MIN AL	56	76	17	15	1	0	1	8	6	20	.197	.262	.250	19
1971	MIN AL	54	93	6	15	3	0	0	5	2	16	.161	.179	.194	18
1972	MIN AL	24	45	3	13	3	0	2	4	1	16	.289	.304	.489	22
1973	MIN AL	31	0	1	0	0	0	0	0	0	0	—	—	—	0
	CHI AL	7	0	0	0	0	0	0	0	0	0	—	—	—	0
	TOTAL	38	0	1	0	0	0	0	0	0	0	—	—	—	0
1974	CHI AL	42	1	0	0	0	0	0	0	0	0	.000	.000	.000	0
1976	PHI NL	42	79	4	14	3	1	1	8	2	24	.177	.195	.278	22
1977	PHI NL	36	53	4	10	3	0	0	2	2	12	.189	.218	.245	13
1978	PHI NL	26	48	4	7	1	0	0	4	0	15	.146	.163	.167	8
1979	PHI NL	3	1	0	0	0	0	0	0	0	1	.000	.500	.000	0
	NY A	40	0	0	0	0	0	0	0	0	0	—	—	—	0
	TOTAL	43	1	0	0	0	0	0	0	0	1	.000	.500	.000	0
1980	NY A	4	0	0	0	0	0	0	0	0	0	—	—	—	0
	STL NL	49	35	4	5	1	0	1	2	2	13	.143	.189	.257	9
	TOT	53	35	4	5	1	0	1	2	2	13	.143	.189	.257	9
1981	STL NL	41	8	2	3	1	0	0	2	1	0	.375	.444	.500	4
1982	STL NL	62	12	0	0	0	0	0	0	1	4	.000	.077	.000	0
1983	STL NL	24	4	0	0	0	0	0	0	0	2	.000	.000	.000	0
25 Yrs.		**1004**	**1251**	**117**	**232**	**44**	**5**	**16**	**106**	**63**	**367**	**.185**	**.227**	**.267**	**334**

* Kaat had no at-bats in 1975.

Jeff Lahti

Year	Team	G	AB	R	H	2B	3B	HR	RBI	SB	BB	SO	BA	OBP	SLG	TB
1982	STL NL	33	13	0	1	0	0	0	0	0	0	8	.077	.077	.077	1
1983	STL NL	53	10	0	0	0	0	0	0	0	0	5	.000	.000	.000	0
1984	STL NL	63	6	0	1	0	0	0	0	0	0	2	.167	.167	.167	1
1985	STL NL	52	9	0	0	0	0	0	0	0	0	5	.000	.000	.000	0
5 Yrs.		**205**	**38**	**0**	**2**	**0**	**0**	**0**	**0**	**0**	**0**	**20**	**.053**	**.053**	**.053**	**2**

* Lahti had no at-bats in 1986.

Tito Landrum

Year	Team	G	AB	R	H	2B	3B	HR	RBI	SB	BB	SO	BA	OBP	SLG	TB
1980	STL NL	35	77	6	19	2	2	0	7	3	6	17	.247	.306	.325	25
1981	STL NL	81	119	13	31	5	4	0	10	4	6	14	.261	.297	.370	44
1982	STL NL	79	72	12	20	3	0	2	14	0	8	18	.278	.358	.403	29
1983	STL NL	6	5	0	1	0	1	0	0	1	1	2	.200	.333	.600	3
	BAL AL	26	42	8	13	2	0	1	4	0	1	11	.310	.318	.429	18
	TOTAL	32	47	8	14	2	1	1	4	1	2	13	.298	.320	.447	21
1984	STL NL	105	173	21	47	9	1	3	26	3	10	27	.272	.306	.387	67
1985	STL NL	85	161	21	45	8	2	4	21	1	19	30	.280	.356	.429	69
1986	STL NL	96	205	24	43	7	1	2	17	3	20	41	.210	.279	.283	58
1987	STL NL	30	50	5	10	1	0	0	6	1	7	14	.200	.298	.220	11
	LA NL	51	67	8	16	3	0	1	4	1	3	16	.239	.282	.328	22
	TOTAL	81	117	13	26	4	0	1	10	2	10	30	.222	.289	.282	33
1988	BAL AL	13	24	2	3	0	1	0	2	0	4	6	.125	.250	.208	5
9 Yrs.		607	995	120	248	40	12	13	111	17	85	196	.249	.309	.353	351

Dave LaPoint*

Year	Team	G	AB	R	H	2B	3B	HR	RBI	SB	BB	SO	BA	OBP	SLG	TB
1981	STL NL	3	5	0	0	0	0	0	0	0	0	3	.000	.000	.000	0
1982	STL NL	42	38	2	2	0	0	0	1	0	1	18	.053	.077	.053	2
1983	STL NL	37	59	4	9	0	0	0	5	0	7	20	.153	.242	.153	9
1984	STL NL	33	59	3	4	0	0	0	3	0	2	19	.068	.097	.068	4
1985	SF NL	31	60	4	10	1	0	0	6	0	6	11	.167	.242	.183	11
1986	SD NL	24	8	0	0	0	0	0	0	0	0	1	.000	.000	.000	0
1987	STL NL	6	4	0	0	0	0	0	0	0	0	3	.000	.000	.000	0
1988	PIT NL	8	16	0	1	0	0	0	0	0	0	6	.062	.062	.062	1
1991	PHI NL	2	2	0	0	0	0	0	0	0	0	1	.000	.000	.000	0
12 Yrs.		**294**	**251**	**13**	**26**	**1**	**0**	**0**	**15**	**0**	**16**	**82**	**.104**	**.157**	**.108**	**27**

* LaPoint played for the Milwaukee Brewers in 1980, but had no at-bats. He played for the American League (and had no at-bats) 1989–1990.

Mark Littell*

Year	Team	G	AB	R	H	2B	3B	HR	RBI	SB	BB	SO	BA	OBP	SLG	TB
1976	KC AL	60	1	0	0	0	0	0	0	0	0	1	.000	.000	.000	0
1977	KC AL	48	1	0	0	0	0	0	0	0	0	1	.000	.000	.000	0
1978	STL NL	72	7	0	0	0	0	0	0	0	1	1	.000	.125	.000	0
1979	STL NL	63	14	1	0	0	0	0	1	0	1	11	.000	.067	.000	0
1980	STL NL	14	1	0	0	0	0	0	0	0	0	0	.000	.000	.000	0
1981	STL NL	28	8	0	2	0	0	0	2	0	0	2	.250	.250	.250	2
1982	STL NL	16	2	0	0	0	0	0	0	0	0	2	.000	.000	.000	0
9 Yrs.		**316**	**34**	**1**	**2**	**0**	**0**	**0**	**3**	**0**	**2**	**18**	**.059**	**.111**	**.059**	**2**

* Littell had no at-bats in 1973 and 1975.

John Martin

Year	Team	G	AB	R	H	2B	3B	HR	RBI	SB	BB	SO	BA	OBP	SLG	TB
1980	STL NL	9	11	0	3	0	0	0	1	0	1	3	.273	.308	.273	3
1981	STL NL	18	33	2	7	2	1	0	8	0	2	14	.212	.257	.333	11
1982	STL NL	24	11	1	1	0	0	0	0	0	1	3	.091	.167	.091	1
1983	STL NL	26	18	1	4	1	0	0	4	0	0	2	.222	.222	.278	5
	DET AL	15	0	0	0	0	0	0	0	0	0	0	—	—	—	0
	TOTAL	41	18	1	4	1	0	0	4	0	0	2	.222	.222	.278	5
4 Yrs.		92	73	4	15	3	1	0	13	0	4	22	.205	.244	.274	25

Willie McGee

Year	Team	G	AB	R	H	2B	3B	HR	RBI	SB	BB	SO	BA	OBP	SLG	TB
1982	STL NL	123	422	43	125	12	8	4	56	24	12	58	.296	.318	.391	165
1983	STL NL	147	601	75	172	22	8	5	75	39	26	98	.286	.314	.374	225
1984	STL NL	145	571	82	166	19	11	6	50	43	29	80	.291	.325	.394	225
1985	STL NL	152	612	114	216	26	18	10	82	56	34	86	.353	.384	.503	308
1986	STL NL	124	497	65	127	22	7	7	48	19	37	82	.256	.306	.370	184
1987	STL NL	153	620	76	177	37	11	11	105	16	24	90	.285	.312	.434	269
1988	STL NL	137	562	73	164	24	6	3	50	41	32	84	.292	.329	.372	209
1989	STL NL	58	199	23	47	10	2	3	17	8	10	34	.236	.275	.352	70
1990	STL NL	125	501	76	168	32	5	3	62	28	38	86	.335	.382	.437	219
	OAK AL	29	113	23	31	3	2	0	15	3	10	18	.274	.333	.336	38
	TOTAL	154	614	99	199	35	7	3	77	31	48	104	.324	.373	.419	257
1991	SF NL	131	497	67	155	30	3	4	43	17	34	74	.312	.357	.408	203
1992	SF NL	138	474	56	141	20	2	1	36	13	29	88	.297	.339	.354	168
1993	SF NL	130	475	53	143	28	1	4	46	10	38	67	.301	.353	.389	185
1994	SF NL	45	156	19	44	3	0	5	23	3	15	24	.282	.337	.397	62
1995	BOS AL	67	200	32	57	11	3	2	15	5	9	41	.285	.311	.400	80
1996	STL NL	123	309	52	95	15	2	5	41	5	18	60	.307	.348	.417	129
1997	STL NL	122	300	29	90	19	4	3	38	8	22	59	.300	.347	.420	126
1998	STL NL	120	269	27	68	10	1	3	34	7	14	49	.253	.287	.331	89
1999	STL NL	132	271	25	68	7	0	0	20	7	17	60	.251	.293	.277	75
18 Yrs.		2201	7649	1010	2254	350	94	79	856	352	448	1238	.295	.333	.396	3029

Steve Mura*

Year	Team	G	AB	R	H	2B	3B	HR	RBI	SB	BB	SO	BA	OBP	SLG	TB
1978	SD NL	5	1	0	0	0	0	0	0	0	0	0	.000	.000	.000	0
1979	SD NL	38	10	1	0	0	0	0	0	0	0	5	.000	.000	.000	0
1980	SD NL	39	51	3	7	2	0	0	8	0	3	21	.137	.185	.176	9
1981	SD NL	24	44	2	6	1	0	0	4	0	2	7	.136	.174	.159	7
1982	STL NL	35	53	3	3	0	0	0	3	0	1	10	.057	.091	.057	3
7 Yrs.		170	159	9	16	3	0	0	15	0	6	43	.101	.139	.119	19

* Mura had no at-bats in 1983 and 1985.

Ken Oberkfell

Year	Team	G	AB	R	H	2B	3B	HR	RBI	SB	BB	SO	BA	OBP	SLG	TB
1977	STL NL	9	9	0	1	0	0	0	1	0	0	3	.111	.111	.111	1
1978	STL NL	24	50	7	6	1	0	0	0	0	3	1	.120	.170	.140	7
1979	STL NL	135	369	53	111	19	5	1	35	4	57	35	.301	.396	.388	143
1980	STL NL	116	422	58	128	27	6	3	46	4	51	23	.303	.377	.417	176
1981	STL NL	102	376	43	110	12	6	2	45	13	37	28	.293	.353	.372	140
1982	STL NL	137	470	55	136	22	5	2	34	11	40	31	.289	.345	.370	174
1983	STL NL	151	488	62	143	26	5	3	38	12	61	27	.293	.371	.385	188
1984	STL NL	50	152	17	47	11	1	0	11	1	16	10	.309	.379	.395	60
	ATL NL	50	172	21	40	8	1	1	10	1	15	17	.233	.289	.308	53
	TOTAL	100	324	38	87	19	2	1	21	2	31	27	.269	.331	.349	113
1985	ATL NL	134	412	30	112	19	4	3	35	1	51	38	.272	.359	.359	148
1986	ATL NL	151	503	62	136	24	3	5	48	7	83	40	.270	.373	.360	181
1987	ATL NL	135	508	59	142	29	2	3	48	3	48	29	.280	.342	.362	184
1988	ATL NL	120	422	42	117	20	4	3	40	4	32	28	.277	.325	.365	154
	PIT NL	20	54	7	12	2	0	0	2	0	5	6	.222	.288	.259	14
	TOTAL	140	476	49	129	22	4	3	42	4	37	34	.271	.321	.353	168
1989	PIT NL	14	40	2	5	1	0	0	2	0	2	2	.125	.163	.150	6
	SF NL	83	116	17	37	5	1	2	15	0	8	8	.319	.367	.431	50
	TOTAL	97	156	19	42	6	1	2	17	0	10	10	.269	.316	.359	56
1990	HOU NL	77	150	10	31	6	1	1	12	1	15	17	.207	.281	.280	42
1991	HOU NL	53	70	7	16	4	0	0	14	0	14	8	.229	.357	.286	20
1992	CAL AL	41	91	6	24	1	0	0	10	0	8	5	.264	.317	.275	25
16 Yrs.		1602	4874	558	1354	237	44	29	446	62	546	356	.278	.351	.362	1766

Kelly Paris

Year	Team	G	AB	R	H	2B	3B	HR	RBI	SB	BB	SO	BA	OBP	SLG	TB
1982	STL NL	12	29	1	3	0	0	0	1	0	0	7	.103	.100	.103	3
1983	CIN NL	56	120	13	30	6	0	0	7	8	15	22	.250	.336	.300	36
1985	BAL AL	5	9	0	0	0	0	0	0	0	0	1	.000	.000	.000	0
1986	BAL AL	5	10	0	2	0	0	0	0	0	0	3	.200	.200	.200	2
1988	CHI AL	14	44	6	11	0	0	3	6	0	0	6	.250	.250	.455	20
5 Yrs.		**92**	**212**	**20**	**46**	**6**	**0**	**3**	**14**	**8**	**15**	**39**	**.217**	**.270**	**.288**	**61**

Darrell Porter

Year	Team	G	AB	R	H	2B	3B	HR	RBI	SB	BB	SO	BA	OBP	SLG	TB
1971	MIL AL	22	70	4	15	2	0	2	9	2	9	20	.214	.300	.329	23
1972	MIL AL	18	56	2	7	1	0	1	2	0	5	21	.125	.210	.196	11
1973	MIL AL	117	350	50	89	19	2	16	67	5	57	85	.254	.363	.457	160
1974	MIL AL	131	432	59	104	15	4	12	56	8	50	88	.241	.326	.377	163
1975	MIL AL	130	409	66	95	12	5	18	60	2	89	77	.232	.371	.418	171
1976	MIL AL	119	389	43	81	14	1	5	32	2	51	61	.208	.298	.288	112
1977	KC AL	130	425	61	117	21	3	16	60	1	53	70	.275	.353	.452	192
1978	KC AL	150	520	77	138	27	6	18	78	0	75	75	.265	.358	.444	231
1979	KC AL	157	533	101	155	23	10	20	112	3	121	65	.291	.421	.484	258
1980	KC AL	118	418	51	104	14	2	7	51	1	69	50	.249	.354	.342	143
1981	STL NL	61	174	22	39	10	2	6	31	1	39	32	.224	.364	.408	71
1982	STL NL	120	373	46	86	18	5	12	48	1	66	66	.231	.347	.402	150
1983	STL NL	145	443	57	116	24	3	15	66	1	68	94	.262	.363	.431	191
1984	STL NL	127	422	56	98	16	3	11	68	5	60	79	.232	.331	.363	153
1985	STL NL	84	240	30	53	12	2	10	36	6	41	48	.221	.335	.412	99
1986	TEX AL	68	155	21	41	6	0	12	29	1	22	51	.265	.360	.535	83
1987	TEX AL	85	130	19	31	3	0	7	21	0	30	43	.238	.387	.423	55
17 Yrs.		**1782**	**5539**	**765**	**1369**	**237**	**48**	**188**	**826**	**39**	**905**	**1025**	**.247**	**.354**	**.409**	**2226**

Mike Ramsey

Year	Team	G	AB	R	H	2B	3B	HR	RBI	SB	BB	SO	BA	OBP	SLG	TB
1978	STL NL	12	5	4	1	0	0	0	0	0	0	1	.200	.200	.200	1
1980	STL NL	59	126	11	33	8	1	0	8	0	3	17	.262	.279	.341	43
1981	STL NL	47	124	19	32	3	0	0	9	4	8	16	.258	.303	.282	35
1982	STL NL	112	256	18	59	8	2	1	21	6	22	34	.230	.294	.289	74
1983	STL NL	97	175	25	46	4	3	1	16	4	12	23	.263	.309	.337	59
1984	STL NL	21	15	1	1	1	0	0	0	0	1	3	.067	.125	.133	2
	MON NL	37	70	2	15	1	0	0	3	0	0	13	.214	.214	.229	16
	TOTAL	58	85	3	16	2	0	0	3	0	1	16	.188	.198	.212	18
1985	LA NL	9	15	1	2	1	0	0	0	0	2	4	.133	.235	.200	3
7 Yrs.		394	786	81	189	26	6	2	57	14	48	111	.240	.285	.296	233

Eric Rasmussen*

Year	Team	G	AB	R	H	2B	3B	HR	RBI	SB	BB	SO	BA	OBP	SLG	TB
1975	STL NL	14	26	1	4	0	0	0	3	0	1	8	.154	.185	.154	4
1976	STL NL	43	38	0	4	1	0	0	2	0	2	15	.105	.150	.132	5
1977	STL NL	34	72	4	10	5	0	0	3	0	5	27	.139	.195	.208	15
1978	STL NL	10	18	1	2	0	0	0	1	0	0	8	.111	.111	.111	2
	SD NL	27	46	0	7	0	0	0	1	0	0	10	.152	.152	.152	7
	TOTAL	37	64	1	9	0	0	0	2	0	0	18	.141	.141	.141	9
1979	SD NL	46	36	1	2	0	0	0	0	0	3	7	.056	.128	.056	2
1980	SD NL	40	21	0	2	2	0	0	0	0	0	8	.095	.095	.190	4
1982	STL NL	8	3	0	0	0	0	0	0	0	1	1	.000	.250	.000	0
8 Yrs.		**239**	**260**	**7**	**31**	**8**	**0**	**0**	**10**	**0**	**12**	**84**	**.119**	**.158**	**.150**	**39**

* Rasmussen had no at-bats in 1983.

Andy Rincon

Year	Team	G	AB	R	H	2B	3B	HR	RBI	SB	BB	SO	BA	OBP	SLG	TB
1980	STL NL	4	12	0	3	0	0	0	1	0	0	5	.250	.250	.250	3
1981	STL NL	5	13	1	3	1	0	0	5	0	1	6	.231	.286	.308	4
1982	STL NL	11	10	3	1	0	0	0	1	0	1	6	.100	.182	.100	1
3 Yrs.		20	35	4	7	1	0	0	7	0	2	17	.200	.243	.229	8

Gene Roof

Year	Team	G	AB	R	H	2B	3B	HR	RBI	SB	BB	SO	BA	OBP	SLG	TB
1981	STL NL	23	60	11	18	6	0	0	3	5	12	16	.300	.411	.400	24
1982	STL NL	11	15	3	4	0	0	0	2	2	1	4	.267	.312	.267	4
1983	STL NL	6	3	1	0	0	0	0	0	0	0	0	.000	.000	.000	0
	MON NL	8	12	2	2	2	0	0	1	0	1	3	.167	.231	.333	4
	TOTAL	14	15	3	2	2	0	0	1	0	1	3	.133	.188	.267	4
3 Yrs.		**48**	**90**	**17**	**24**	**8**	**0**	**0**	**6**	**7**	**14**	**23**	**.267**	**.362**	**.356**	**32**

Orlando Sanchez

Year	Team	G	AB	R	H	2B	3B	HR	RBI	SB	BB	SO	BA	OBP	SLG	TB
1981	STL NL	27	49	5	14	2	1	0	6	1	2	6	.286	.308	.367	18
1982	STL NL	26	37	6	7	0	1	0	3	0	5	5	.189	.286	.243	9
1983	STL NL	6	6	0	0	0	0	0	0	0	0	4	.000	.000	.000	0
1984	BAL AL	4	8	0	2	0	0	0	1	0	0	2	.250	.250	.250	2
	KC AL	10	10	0	1	1	0	0	2	0	0	2	.100	.100	.200	2
	TOTAL	14	18	0	3	1	0	0	3	0	0	4	.167	.167	.222	4
4 Yrs.		73	110	11	24	3	2	0	12	1	7	19	.218	.263	.282	31

Lonnie Smith

Year	Team	G	AB	R	H	2B	3B	HR	RBI	SB	BB	SO	BA	OBP	SLG	TB
1978	PHI NL	17	4	6	0	0	0	0	0	4	4	3	.000	.500	.000	0
1979	PHI NL	17	30	4	5	2	0	0	3	2	1	7	.167	.194	.233	7
1980	PHI NL	100	298	69	101	14	4	3	20	33	26	48	.339	.397	.443	132
1981	PHI NL	62	176	40	57	14	3	2	11	21	18	14	.324	.402	.472	83
1982	STL NL	156	592	120	182	35	8	8	69	68	64	74	.307	.381	.434	257
1983	STL NL	130	492	83	158	31	5	8	45	43	41	55	.321	.381	.453	223
1984	STL NL	145	504	77	126	20	4	6	49	50	70	90	.250	.349	.341	172
1985	STL NL	28	96	15	25	2	2	0	7	12	15	20	.260	.377	.323	31
	KC AL	120	448	77	115	23	4	6	41	40	41	69	.257	.321	.366	164
	TOTAL	148	544	92	140	25	6	6	48	52	56	89	.257	.332	.358	195
1986	KC AL	134	508	80	146	25	7	8	44	26	46	78	.287	.357	.411	209
1987	KC AL	48	167	26	42	7	1	3	8	9	24	31	.251	.355	.359	60
1988	ATL NL	43	114	14	27	3	0	3	9	4	10	25	.237	.296	.342	39
1989	ATL NL	134	482	89	152	34	4	21	79	25	76	95	.315	.415	.533	257
1990	ATL NL	135	466	72	142	27	9	9	42	10	58	69	.305	.384	.459	214
1991	ATL NL	122	353	58	97	19	1	7	44	9	50	64	.275	.377	.394	139
1992	ATL NL	84	158	23	39	8	2	6	33	4	17	37	.247	.324	.437	69
1993	PIT NL	94	199	35	57	5	4	6	24	9	43	42	.286	.422	.442	88
	BAL AL	9	24	8	5	1	0	2	3	0	8	10	.208	.406	.500	12
	TOTAL	103	223	43	62	6	4	8	27	9	51	52	.278	.420	.448	100
1994	BAL AL	35	59	13	12	3	0	0	2	1	11	18	.203	.333	.254	15
17 Yrs.		**1613**	**5170**	**909**	**1488**	**27**	**58**	**98**	**533**	**370**	**623**	**849**	**.288**	**.371**	**.420**	**2171**

Ozzie Smith

Year	Team	G	AB	R	H	2B	3B	HR	RBI	SB	BB	SO	BA	OBP	SLG	TB
1978	SD NL	159	590	69	152	17	6	1	46	40	47	43	.258	.311	.312	184
1979	SD NL	156	587	77	124	18	6	0	27	28	37	37	.211	.260	.262	154
1980	SD NL	158	609	67	140	18	5	0	35	57	71	49	.230	.313	.276	168
1981	SD NL	110	450	53	100	11	2	0	21	22	41	37	.222	.294	.256	115
1982	STL NL	140	488	58	121	24	1	2	43	25	68	32	.248	.339	.314	153
1983	STL NL	159	552	69	134	30	6	3	50	34	64	36	.243	.321	.335	185
1984	STL NL	124	412	53	106	20	5	1	44	35	56	17	.257	.347	.337	139
1985	STL NL	158	537	70	148	22	3	6	54	31	65	27	.276	.355	.361	194
1986	STL NL	153	514	67	144	19	4	0	54	31	79	27	.280	.376	.333	171
1987	STL NL	158	600	104	182	40	4	0	75	43	89	36	.303	.392	.383	230
1988	STL NL	153	575	80	155	27	1	3	51	57	74	43	.270	.350	.336	193
1989	STL NL	155	593	82	162	30	8	2	50	29	55	37	.273	.335	.361	214
1990	STL NL	143	512	61	130	21	1	1	50	32	61	33	.254	.330	.305	156
1991	STL NL	150	550	96	157	30	3	3	50	35	83	36	.285	.380	.367	202
1992	STL NL	132	518	73	153	20	2	0	31	43	59	34	.295	.367	.342	177
1993	STL NL	141	545	75	157	22	6	1	53	21	43	18	.288	.337	.356	194
1994	STL NL	98	381	51	100	18	3	3	30	6	38	26	.262	.326	.349	133
1995	STL NL	44	156	16	31	5	1	0	11	4	17	12	.199	.282	.244	38
1996	STL NL	82	227	36	64	10	2	2	18	7	25	9	.282	.358	.370	84
19 Yrs.		2573	9396	1257	2460	402	69	28	793	580	1072	589	.262	.337	.328	3084

John Stuper

Year	Team	G	AB	R	H	2B	3B	HR	RBI	SB	BB	SO	BA	OBP	SLG	TB
1982	STL NL	23	42	1	5	0	1	0	0	0	1	24	.119	.140	.167	7
1983	STL NL	40	59	2	8	0	0	0	6	0	4	32	.136	.190	.136	8
1984	STL NL	15	16	0	1	0	0	0	1	0	1	8	.062	.118	.062	1
1985	CIN NL	33	17	0	1	0	0	0	1	1	3	10	.059	.200	.059	1
4 Yrs.		111	134	3	15	0	1	0	8	1	9	74	.112	.168	.127	17

Bruce Sutter

Year	Team	G	AB	R	H	2B	3B	HR	RBI	SB	BB	SO	BA	OBP	SLG	TB
1976	CHI NL	52	8	0	0	0	0	0	0	0	1	6	.000	.111	.000	0
1977	CHI NL	62	20	4	3	0	0	0	0	0	2	10	.150	.227	.150	3
1978	CHI NL	64	13	1	1	0	0	0	0	0	2	8	.077	.200	.077	1
1979	CHI NL	62	12	0	3	0	0	0	3	1	1	5	.250	.308	.250	3
1980	CHI NL	60	9	0	1	0	0	0	1	0	0	6	.111	.111	.111	1
1981	STL NL	48	9	0	0	0	0	0	1	0	0	4	.000	.100	.000	0
1982	STL NL	70	8	1	1	0	0	0	1	0	0	1	.125	.111	.125	1
1983	STL NL	60	7	0	0	0	0	0	0	0	0	4	.000	.000	.000	0
1984	STL NL	71	10	0	0	0	0	0	0	0	0	3	.000	.000	.000	0
1985	ATL NL	58	4	0	0	0	0	0	0	0	0	1	.000	.000	.000	0
1986	ATL NL	16	1	0	0	0	0	0	0	0	0	1	.000	.000	.000	0
1988	ATL NL	38	1	0	0	0	0	0	0	0	1	1	.000	.500	.000	0
12 Yrs.		**661**	**102**	**6**	**9**	**0**	**0**	**0**	**6**	**1**	**7**	**50**	**.088**	**.153**	**.088**	**9**

Gene Tenace

Year	Team	G	AB	R	H	2B	3B	HR	RBI	SB	BB	SO	BA	OBP	SLG	TB
1969	OAK AL	16	38	1	6	0	0	1	2	0	1	15	.158	.200	.237	9
1970	OAK AL	38	105	19	32	6	0	7	20	0	23	30	.305	.430	.562	59
1971	OAK AL	65	179	26	49	7	0	7	25	2	29	34	.274	.381	.430	77
1972	OAK AL	82	227	22	51	5	3	5	32	0	24	42	.225	.307	.339	77
1973	OAK AL	160	510	83	132	18	2	24	84	2	101	94	.259	.387	.443	226
1974	OAK AL	158	484	71	102	17	1	26	73	2	110	105	.211	.367	.411	199
1975	OAK AL	158	498	83	127	17	0	29	87	7	106	127	.255	.395	.464	231
1976	OAK AL	128	417	64	104	19	1	22	66	5	81	91	.249	.373	.458	191
1977	SD NL	147	437	66	102	24	4	15	61	5	125	119	.233	.415	.410	179
1978	SD NL	142	401	60	90	18	4	16	61	6	101	98	.224	.392	.409	164
1979	SD NL	151	463	61	122	16	4	20	67	2	105	106	.263	.403	.445	206
1980	SD NL	133	316	46	70	11	1	17	50	4	92	63	.222	.399	.424	134
1981	STL NL	58	129	26	30	7	0	5	22	0	38	26	.233	.416	.403	52
1982	STL NL	66	124	18	32	9	0	7	18	1	36	31	.258	.436	.500	62
1983	PIT NL	53	62	7	11	5	0	0	6	0	12	17	.177	.346	.258	16
15 Yrs.		**1555**	**4390**	**653**	**1060**	**179**	**20**	**201**	**674**	**36**	**984**	**998**	**.241**	**.388**	**.429**	**1882**

Index

A

ABC's *World News Tonight*, 54
Adirondack Lumberjacks, 64, 70
African-American managers, 23
alcohol abuse. *See also* drug
    abuse
  and Green, 18
  and Darrell Porter, 89
Alou, Felipe, 3
American League, 104
Andujar, Christopher, 2
Andujar, Jesse, 2
Andujar, Joaquin, 1–8
  Herzog on, ix, xi
  injury, 141–43, 145–46
  in 1982 World Series, Game 3,
      68, 138, 141–43,
      145–46
  in 1982 World Series, Game 6,
      153
  in 1982 World Series, Game 7,
      157–59
  in rotation, 65
  statistics, 162, 178, 210
Aparicio, Luis, 108
Arkansas, Double A, 71
Aspromonte, Ken, 22
Atlanta Braves
  B. Forsch against, 9
  A. Herr drafted by, 40
  Herzog on, xi–xii
  in National League
      Championship Series,
      1996, 27
  1982 sweep of by St. Louis, 67
  and Oberkfell, 84, 85, 146

  Darrell Porter against, 89
  L. Smith with, 100, 105
  Ozzie Smith against, 110
  and Bruce Sutter, 127–28, 130,
      131
Atlanta, GA, 127–28
autographs, 91

B

Bair, Doug
  Herzog on, ix
  in 1982 World Series, Game 2,
      139
  in 1982 World Series, Game 3,
      143, 145
  statistics, 163, 179
  Stuper on, 123
Baker, Dusty, 77
Baltimore Orioles
  Landrum with, 53, 60
  L. Smith with, 105
Bando, Sal, 154
Barker, Len, 129
Barrett, Michael, 129
baseball camps
  Cardinal Legends, 29
  in Louisiana, MO, 19–20
Baseball Hall of Fame, 107–8, 115
baseball schools
  Joaquin Andujar's, 1–2
  Ozzie Smith's, 114
basketball, 28–29, 41
Bates, Buddy, 32, 70
batting coaches, 27
Bearden, Gene, 156
Bell, Greg, 22, 28

Benedict, Bruce, 84

Benson, Kris, 129

Bonds, Barry, 19

Boras, Scott, 35

Bosley, Freeman R., Jr., 114

Boyer, Clancy, 19

Branch Rickey Award (1994), 113

Braun, Steve

    Herzog on, ix

    in 1982 World Series, Game 2, 137, 139

    in 1982 World Series, Game 7, 159

    statistics, 180

Brett, George, vi, 32

Brock, Lou, 17, 19, 144

Bronner, Jim, 70

Brummer, Glenn, xi

    statistics, 181

Brunansky, Tom, 45

Buck, Jack, 76

Burnes, Robert L., on 1982 World Series, 134–39, 157–60

Burns, Britt, 60

Burroughs, Jeff, 111

Busch, August, Jr., vi, vii, 11, 160

Busch, Mrs., 59

Busch Stadium walls, 18

Bush, George, 124

businesses, small, 113–14

Butler County Community College, 118

C

Caldwell, Mike

    in 1982 World Series, Game 1, 135–36

    in 1982 World Series, Game 5, 149, 151

    in 1982 World Series, Game 7, 159

California Angels

    Joaquin Andujar as scout for, 2–4

    K. Forsch with, 12

    G. Hendrick with, 27

The Californian, 22

Canseco, Jose, 77

Capital City (Columbia, SC), South Atlantic League, 82

Capital Lumber Co., 49

Cardinals Legends Camp, 29

Carty, Rico, 3

change-up pitch, 65–66

charities, 113

chewing tobacco, 95

Chicago Cubs, 44, 84, 130

Chicago White Sox, 69

Cincinnati Reds

    Caldwell with, 135

    in 1972 World Series, 27

    in 1990 World Series, 77

    Stuper with, 118, 123

Clancy Boyer Chevrolet Pontiac & Buick Inc., 19

Clark, Jack

    acquisition of, 19, 68

    against Dodgers, 7

Clayton, Royce, 110

Clearwater, Florida State League, 81–82

Cleveland Indians

    Bearden with, 156

G. Hendrick with, 22, 26
Hernandez with, 35
Clinton, IA, 94
closers, 129–30
CNN-SI, 109
coaching
T. Herr and, 40
Stuper and, 118–19
Coleman, Vince
automatic tarpaulin machine
accident, 60
call up from Louisville, 104
on McGee, 76
Columbia University, 35
Columbus University, 128
Cooper, Cecil
in 1982 World Series, Game 1,
136
in 1982 World Series, Game 2,
138–39
in 1982 World Series, Game 3,
142
in 1982 World Series, Game 4,
145
in 1982 World Series, Game 5,
150
in 1982 World Series, Game 7,
159
Coppenbarger, Frank, 84
Corona Cardinals, 29
Costas, Bob, 112
Crawford, Willie, 135
Cy Young Award, 6

D

D'Acquisto, John, 135
Darcy, Pat, 135

Darling, Ron, 33
Darr, Mike, 95
Davey, Tom, 26
Dawson, Andre, 112
Deer, Rob, 22
Denkinger, Don, 7, 14
Detroit Tigers
LaPoint traded to, 69
in 1968 World Series, 144, 156
The Diamond (Lake Elsinore), 28,
56
dog-grooming business, 17, 20
Dominican Republic, 1–4
drug abuse. *See also* alcohol
abuse
and Hernandez, 33–34
and Darrell Porter, 89
and L. Smith, 99, 102–4
Duckworth, Brandon, 82
Duggan, Hacksaw, 64
Duke University, 41
Durham, Leon, viii, 44, 84

E

Easler, Mike, 27
Ebersol, Dick, 122
Ebersol, Willie, 122
Elmira, NY, independent team in,
81
Evans, Jim
in 1982 World Series, Game 3,
141
in 1982 World Series, Game 6,
154
Everett, Adam, 129

F

failure, T. Herr on, 46–47
faith, of Darrell Porter, 91–92
farm teams. *See* minor league
    baseball
Fayette County, GA, 101
FBI (Federal Bureau of
    Investigation), 33–34,
    99–100, 103
Fernandez, Tony, 3
Fingers, Rollie, 129, 146
Fischer, Peter, 10
Florida, 31, 35
Florida State League, 81–83
Ford, Curt, 17
    at Louisiana, MO, baseball
        camp, 20
    Ozzie Smith on, 111
Forsch, Bob, 9–16
    on Joaquin Andujar, 5
    on G. Hendrick, 22, 27
    Herzog on, ix, xi, 136
    on McGee, 76
    in 1982 World Series, Game 1,
        134, 136
    in 1982 World Series, Game 5,
        148–52
    in rotation, 65
    on Ozzie Smith, 114
    statistics, 164, 182
Forsch, Ken
    on Joaquin Andujar, 5
    with California Angels, 12
Forster, Terry, 60
Foster, Bill, 41
Fox, Helen, xii
Fox, Herb, xii

G

Gall, Bryan, 24
Gantner, Jim
    in 1982 World Series, Game 3,
        142
    in 1982 World Series, Game 6,
        154, 156
    in 1982 World Series, Game 7,
        158–59
Garagiola, Joe
    on McGee, 74
    in 1946 World Series, 135
Garber, Gene, 84
Garvey, Steve, 60
Gieselmann, Gene, 142
Gilhooley, Bob, 70
Glen Falls, NY, 63, 70
Gold Glove
    Joaquin Andujar awarded, 6
    McGee awarded, 76
    Ozzie Smith awarded, 112
Gomez, Andre, 24
Gonzalez, Julio, 183
Gooden, Dwight
    and Cy Young Award, 6
    and drug abuse, 34
Gossage, Goose, 129
Green, David, 17–20
    B. Forsch on, 16
    Herzog on, viii
    injury, 75
    in 1982 World Series, Game 5,
        149–51
    in 1982 World Series, Game 6,
        155

against San Francisco Giants,
xi
statistics, 184

H

Haas, Moose, 144
Hagerstown, MD, 93
Hagerstown Suns, 94
Harkey, Mike, 22
Harvard University, 121–22
Heath, Mike, 8
Hempfield High School, 39
Hendrick, Brian, 29
Hendrick, George, 21–29
    Herzog on, ix, x
    and Lake Elsinore Storm, 2
    in 1982 World Series, Game 2,
        137–39
    in 1982 World Series, Game 3,
        141–42
    in 1982 World Series, Game 5,
        149–50
    in 1982 World Series, Game 6,
        154–55
    in 1982 World Series, Game 7,
        157, 159–60
    statistics, 185
Herman, Jack, 64–65
    on 1982 World Series, Game 3,
        140–43
    on 1982 World Series, Game 5,
        148–52
Hernandez, Keith, 31–38
    LaPoint on, 65
    in left field, vii, 89
    in 1982 World Series, Game 1,
        134, 136

    in 1982 World Series, Game 2,
        138–39
    in 1982 World Series, Game 4,
        67, 145
    in 1982 World Series, Game 5,
        149–51
    in 1982 World Series, Game 6,
        154–55
    in 1982 World Series, Game 7,
        27, 157, 159–60
    Oberkfell on, 84
    statistics, 186
Herr, Aaron, 39–42, 47
Herr, Jeff, 44
Herr, Jordan, 39, 42, 47
Herr, Kim, 39–40
Herr, Tom, 39–47
    on Brewers scouting reports,
        13
    Herzog on, vii, 85
    in 1982 World Series, Game 1,
        136
    in 1982 World Series, Game 2,
        138
    in 1982 World Series, Game 3,
        142
    in 1982 World Series, Game 4,
        146
    in 1982 World Series, Game 6,
        154–55
    in 1982 World Series, Game 7,
        158
    at second base, 32, 83–84
    statistics, 187
Herzog, Mary Lou, xii–xiii

Herzog, Whitey
    and Joaquin Andujar, 2–4, 8,
        141
    and August Busch Jr., 11
    ejection from 1985 World
        Series, 7
    B. Forsch on, 11–12
    on Green, 18
    on G. Hendrick, 27, 159
    and Hernandez, 32
    on T. Herr, 43–44
    on Landrum, 60
    on LaPoint, 65–67
    on McGee, 74, 75, 140
    on 1982 World Series, Game 1,
        136
    on 1982 World Series, Game 2,
        139
    on 1982 World Series, Game 3,
        141
    on 1982 World Series, Game 5,
        149
    on 1982 World Series, Game 7,
        158
    on 1982 season, v–xiii
    and Oberkfell, 83, 85
    on Darrell Porter, 89–90
    Mike Ramsey on, 96
    on L. Smith, 103, 106
    on Ozzie Smith, 108–9, 112
    and Stuper, 65, 118, 121
    on Bruce Sutter, 130
    on Yount, 151
Hiller, Chuck
    Herzog on, x
    in 1982 World Series, Game 6,
        154
hitters, statistics, 177–209
Houston Astros
    Joaquin Andujar with, 4–5, 8
    B. Forsch traded to, 14–15
    Oberkfell on, 85
    St. Louis' defeat of on
        Opening Day, 1982, 65
Houston, TX, 85
Howe, Steve, 102
Howell, Roy, 142, 143
Hrabosky, Al, 77–78
Hummel, Rick, 22
hunting, 127–28
Hurcules, CA, 78
Hyland Center, 103

I

Independence, Little League
    complex in, 90
Iorg, Dane, 49–51
    Herzog on, ix
    in 1982 World Series, Game 2,
        138
    in 1982 World Series, Game 3,
        142
    in 1982 World Series, Game 6,
        155
    statistics, 188
Iorg, Garth, 49–50

J

Javier, Julian, 3
Javier, Stan, 75
John Burroughs school, 10
Johnson, Randy, 112

Jorgensen, Mike, 71
Jupiter, FL, 31

K

Kaat, Jim
    Herzog on, ix
    LaPoint on, 66
    in 1982 World Series, Game 2,
        139
    in 1982 World Series, Game 3,
        143, 145
    in 1982 World Series, Game 6,
        155
    statistics, 165, 189
    Stuper on, 118, 123
    and Bruce Sutter, 131
Kansas City Royals
    broadcasters, 91
    D. Iorg with, 50
    in 1985 World Series, 7, 14
    Darrell Porter with, 89–90
    L. Smith with, 100, 104–5
Keener, Jeff, 166
Kiener Plaza, 114–15
Kissell, George, 83
Kittle, Hub
    Herzog on, x
    LaPoint on, 66, 71
    on trade for Joaquin Andujar,
        4
Koster, Rich, on 1982 World
    Series, 144–47
Kuenn, Harvey
    in 1982 World Series, Game 3,
        142
    in 1982 World Series, Game 4,
        146

in 1982 World Series, Game 6,
    154
in 1982 World Series, Game 7,
    159
Kuhn, Bowie, 154
Kurowski, Whitey, 135

L

Ladd, Peter, 139
Lahti, Jeff
    LaPoint on, 66
    statistics, 167, 190
Lake Elsinore, CA, 24–25
Lake Elsinore Storm, 2, 21–26,
    28–29
Lancaster, PA, 39
Landrum, "Tito" Terry, 53–61
    statistics, 191
landscaping, 101
Langton, Mary Jane, 25
Lanier, Hal, x
LaPoint, Dave, 63–71
    on Joaquin Andujar, 5
    Herzog on, ix
    in 1982 World Series, Game 4,
        145
    statistics, 168, 192
    and Bruce Sutter, 131
Largo, FL, 94
LaRussa, Tony
    and batting coaches, 27
    at Oakland A's, 77
    and Ozzie Smith, 109–10
Las Vegas, NV, 94
Lee's Summit, MO, 87
Littell, Mark, 169, 193
Little Rock, AR, 94

Long Island Ducks, 71

Los Angeles Dodgers
    Landrum with, 53
    Ozzie Smith against, 111
    Stuper against, 118
losing, Hendrick on, 28
Louisiana, MO, 19–20
Lyle, Sparky, 129
Lynch, Ed, 33

M

Madlock, Bill, 65
Marichal, Juan, 3
Marion, Marty, 108
Martin, John
    Herzog on, ix
    statistics, 170, 194
Martinez, Pedro, 3
Maryville, IL, 81
Maxvill, Dal, 45
McClure, Bob
    in 1982 World Series, Game 4,
        146
    in 1982 World Series, Game 5,
        149, 151
    in 1982 World Series, Game 7,
        27, 31, 159
McDonald's restaurants, 88
McEwing, Joe, 97
McGee, Willie, 73–79
    call up from Louisville, 18
    B. Forsch on, 13
    Herzog on, viii
    in 1982 World Series, Game 2,
        138
    in 1982 World Series, Game 3,
        140–42

in 1982 World Series, Game 4,
        146
    in 1982 World Series, Game 5,
        149
    in 1982 World Series, Game 6,
        154–55
    in 1982 World Series, Game 7,
        158, 160
    statistics, 195
McGraw, Tommy, 19
McGraw, Tug, 129
McGwire, Mark, 77, 113
McKeon, Jack, vi
McLure, Bob, 139
McRae, Hal, 105
Meacham, Bobby, 75
media, 22, 28–29
Merkel, Susan, 20
Milwaukee Brewers. *See also*
        World Series, 1982
    and B. Forsch, 9, 12–13
    LaPoint traded to, 69
    Darrell Porter against, 89
    Simmons traded to, 18, 32, 89
Minnesota Twins, 45
minor league baseball. *See also*
specific teams
    G. Hendrick as manager in, 24
    Oberkfell as manager in,
        81–83
    Mike Ramsey as manager in,
        93–97
    Bruce Sutter as coach in, 128
Mobile, AL, 94

Molitor, Paul
  in 1982 World Series, Game 1, 135, 136
  in 1982 World Series, Game 2, 138
  in 1982 World Series, Game 3, 74, 141–42
  in 1982 World Series, Game 5, 149–51
  in 1982 World Series, Game 6, 156
  in 1982 World Series, Game 7, 158–59
Money, Don, 143
Montreal Expos
  LaPoint against, 67
  Stuper with, 118–19
Moody, Sterling, 114
Moore, Charlie
  in 1982 World Series, Game 1, 136
  in 1982 World Series, Game 2, 138
  in 1982 World Series, Game 3, 142–43
  on 1982 World Series, Game 5, 150–51
Mota, Manny, 3
Mura, Steve, 171, 196
Murphy, Dale, 99
MVP awards
  National League, 1982, 99, 106
  National League, 1985, 76
  Darrell Porter's, 89–90
  World Series, 1982, 92

N

NAACP Image Award, 113
National League MVP award
  1982, 99, 106
  1985, 76
National League Rookie of the Year, 2001, 82
New Haven, CT, 71
New York City
  Hernandez in, 33, 38
  Landrum in, 54–61
New York Mets
  Hernandez with, 31–34, 37–38
  T. Herr traded to, 45
  Oberkfell with, 81, 82
  Mike Ramsey against, 96
  television broadcast crew of, 36
New York University, 54–56
New York University baseball team, 58
New York Yankees
  LaPoint with, 64, 69
  McGee with, 75, 140
  C. Sutter drafted by, 128
nicknames, 67
Niekro, Phil, xii
no-hitters, 14

O

Oakland A's
  Joaquin Andujar traded to, 8
  G. Hendrick with, 27
  McGee traded to, 77
Oberkfell, Ken, 81–86
  Herzog on, vii

in 1982 World Series, Game 1,
135

in 1982 World Series, Game 2,
138–39

in 1982 World Series, Game 3,
5, 143

in 1982 World Series, Game 4,
145, 146

in 1982 World Series, Game 5,
148–50

in 1982 World Series, Game 6,
155

in 1982 World Series, Game 7,
159

statistics, 197

at third base, 32, 44

Oberkfell, Tina, 85–86

O'Connell, Jack, 107

O'Fallon, MO, 114

Oglivie, Ben

in 1982 World Series, Game 1,
136

in 1982 World Series, Game 3,
143

in 1982 World Series, Game 4,
67, 145

in 1982 World Series, Game 5,
149

in 1982 World Series, Game 6,
154

in 1982 World Series, Game 7,
158

Olympic torch, 114–15

Opening Day, 1982, 64–65

Orangeburg, SC, 53

Orlando, FL, 94

Orta, Jorge, 7

Oster, David, 23

Ozzie Smith's Sports Academy,
114

Ozzie's (sports bar), 113

P

Page, Mitchell, 27

Pallone, Dave, xi

Palmer, Dave, 63

Paris, Kelly, 198

Parker, Dave, 27

Patkin, Max, 71

Patterson, Corey, 128–29

Pauley, Jane, 122

Pawtucket, Boston Triple A, 77

Peña, Tony, 3

Pendleton, Terry, 38, 85

pennant race, 1982, xi–xii

Perez, Ellis, 3

Philadelphia Phillies

affiliate teams, 81–82

T. Herr traded to, 45

Herzog on 1982 game with, xi

LaPoint traded to, 69

in 1983 World Series, 60

and Oberkfell, 82

Bruce Sutter against, 130

Phillips, Dave, 141–42

physical therapy, 54–58

Piedmont Class A South Atlantic
League, 81

Piniella, Lou, 77

pitchers

relief, 129–30

statistics, 161–75

Pitchers (bar and restaurant), 64, 70–71

pitching
  G. Hendrick on, 23–24
  LaPoint on, 65

Pittsburgh, PA, 33, 100, 102

Pittsburgh Pirates
  and LaPoint, 65, 69
  L. Smith with, 105

Plus One, 56–57

Podres, Johnny, 63

Pomeray, Adrian, 22

Port St. Lucie, FL, 81

Porter, Darrell, 87–92
  D. Iorg on, 50
  in 1982 World Series, Game 1, 135, 138
  in 1982 World Series, Game 2, 137, 139
  in 1982 World Series, Game 3, 142
  in 1982 World Series, Game 5, 151
  in 1982 World Series, Game 6, 154–55
  in 1982 World Series, Game 7, xii, 123, 159–60
  signing of, vii
  statistics, 199
  Stuper on, 123

Porter, Deanne, 89

Porter, Jeff, 90

Porter, Lindsey, 90, 92

Porter, Ryan, 90

Proverbs 3:5–6, 91

Pujols, Albert, 82

R

Ramirez, Manny, 3

Ramsey, Jordan, 97

Ramsey, Matt, 97

Ramsey, Merle, 97

Ramsey, Mike, 93–97
  Herzog on, ix
  in 1982 World Series, Game 7, 159
  at shortstop, xi
  statistics, 200

Rancho Cucamonga Quakes, 2

Rasmussen, Eric
  Herzog on, ix
  statistics, 172, 201

Reitz, Ken, vii, 44, 84

relief pitchers, 129–30

Richard, J. R., 130

Ricketts, Dave, x

Rijo, Jose, 3

Rincon, Andy
  Herzog on, ix
  statistics, 173, 202

Roberto Clemente Award, 1995, 113

Robinson, Frank, 26

Rollins, Jimmy, 82

Roof, Gene, 203

Rose, Pete, 119, 121

Ryan, Nolan, x, 65, 130

S

St. Albans, MO, 107

St. Claire, Randy, 63

St. Louis
  B. Forsch on, 15
  D. Iorg on, 51

LaPoint on, 68
Darrell Porter on, 89
L. Smith on, 104
Ozzie Smith on, 113
St. Louis Man of the Year Award, 113
St. Louis Municipal Opera, 114
St. Louis Regional Commerce and Growth Association, 113
St. Petersburg, FL, 94
San Diego Padres
D. Iorg with, 49
LaPoint traded to, 69
Mike Ramsey with, 94, 97
Ozzie Smith with, 108, 111
San Francisco Giants
Caldwell with, 135
Clayton with, 110
Green with, 19
T. Herr traded to, 45
Herzog on 1982 game with, xi
LaPoint traded to, 68
McGee with, 77, 79
Mike Ramsey with, 94
San Pedro de Macoris, 1–3
Sanchez, Orlando, 204
Savannah, GA, 94
Schmidt, Mike, 130
Schoendienst, Red, x
Schuerholz, John, 100, 105
Scott, Tony, 4
Seattle Mariners, 112
Seinfeld, 35–36
September 11, 2001, terrorist attacks
Hernandez on, 38

Landrum on, 56–57
Shannon, Mike, 68
Simmons, Ted
at Cardinals' Class A team, 93
at first base, 89
in 1982 World Series, Game 1, 134, 135, 136
in 1982 World Series, Game 2, 137, 138–39
in 1982 World Series, Game 3, 5, 141–42, 145, 157
in 1982 World Series, Game 5, 149–50, 152
in 1982 World Series, Game 6, 154
in 1982 World Series, Game 7, 160
popularity of, vii
Mike Ramsey on, 96
Bruce Sutter on, 132
trade to Milwaukee, 18, 32, 89
Slaughter, Enos, 135
Slay, David, 113
Slippery Rock University, 119
Smith and Slay's (restaurant), 113
Smith, Dorothy, 101
Smith, Dustin, 111
Smith, Lonnie, 99–106
in 1982 World Series, Game 2, 138, 139
in 1982 World Series, Game 3, 141–42
in 1982 World Series, Game 5, 149–51
in 1982 World Series, Game 6, 154–55

in 1982 World Series, Game 7, 157–60

statistics, 205

Smith, O. J., 111

Smith, Ozzie, 107–15

Joaquin Andujar on, 6

on Brewers scouting reports, 13

B. Forsch on, 16

Herzog on, vi, viii

injury, xi, 96

D. Iorg on, 50

and McGee, 13, 76, 78

in 1982 World Series, Game 3, 142

in 1982 World Series, Game 4, 146

in 1982 World Series, Game 5, 150

in 1982 World Series, Game 7, 157, 159–60

Oberkfell on, 84

at shortstop, 32

L. Smith on, 106

statistics, 206

Smith, Tarya, 111

Sosa, Sammy, 3

Soto, Mario, 3, 22–23

South Atlantic League

Oberkfell with, 81–82

Mike Ramsey with, 94

Sowers, Josh, 117–18

Spartanburg, SC, 105

split-fingered fastball, 129

Sporting News Silver Bat, 16

Springfield, IL, 93–94, 95

Stargell, Willie, 37

Staub, Rusty, 33

Steinbrenner, George, 75

Stengel, Casey, viii

Sterling's Market, 114

Strawberry, Darryl

against Cardinals, 37–38

and drug abuse, 34

strike, 1981, 12

Stuper, John, 117–25

Herzog on, ix

in 1982 World Series, Game 1, 134

in 1982 World Series, Game 2, 138–39

in 1982 World Series, Game 6, xii, 13–14, 153, 155–56

against Philadelphia Phillies, 1982, xi

in rotation, 65

statistics, 174, 207

and Bruce Sutter, 131

Stuper, Pam, 122–23

Stutz, Bill, 88, 91

Sullivan County, NY, 81

Sutcliffe, Rick, 6

Sutter, Ben, 128

Sutter, Bruce, 121–32

acquisition of, viii, 84

and Cy Young Award, 6

LaPoint on, 66

in 1982 World Series, Game 2, 137, 138, 139

in 1982 World Series, Game 3, 5, 141, 143, 145–46

in 1982 World Series, Game 5, 148, 151

in 1982 World Series, Game 7, xii, 37, 68, 74, 123, 157–60

on party at B. Forsch's, 9–10

against Philadelphia Phillies, 1982, xi

statistics, 175, 208

Stuper on, 123

trade for, 44

Sutter, Chad, 128–29

Sutter, Josh, 128

Sutton, Don

in 1982 World Series, Game 1, 134

in 1982 World Series, Game 2, 138–39

in 1982 World Series, Game 6, 153–55

Sykes, Bob, 75, 76, 140

T

Tampa Bay Devil Rays, 94

Tarnoff, Larry, 141

Tekulve, Kent, 129

television, Hernandez on, 35–36

Templeton, Garry

Mike Ramsey on, 96

trade of, vi, viii

Tenace, Gene

Herzog on, ix

LaPoint on, 65

in 1982 World Series, Game 4, 146

in 1982 World Series, Game 5, 148–49

in 1982 World Series, Game 7, 159

statistics, 209

and Bruce Sutter, 131

Texas

Oberkfell in, 83

Darrell Porter in, 90

Thomas, Gorman

in 1982 World Series, Game 1, 136

in 1982 World Series, Game 2, 138

in 1982 World Series, Game 3, 142–43

in 1982 World Series, Game 4, 145

in 1982 World Series, Game 5, 150

in 1982 World Series, Game 6, 13–14

in 1982 World Series, Game 7, xii, 37, 68, 74, 132, 157, 160

Stuper on, 123

Toronto Blue Jays, 50

Torre, Joe, 109, 146

Trudeau, Garry, 122

Tulane University, 128

U

Ueberroth, Peter, 100, 104–5

University of Delaware, 41

V

Van Slyke, Andy, 22–23

A View from Second Base (Herr), 46

Vuckovich, Pete
  in 1982 World Series, Game 3,
      74, 138, 140–42
  in 1982 World Series, Game 6,
      153
  in 1982 World Series, Game 7,
      158–59

W

Wallace Field, 20
Walter Payton Sweetness Award,
    2001, 113
"Whiteyball," x, 134, 158
Wichita, KS, 94
Williams, Carol, 54, 56, 57, 59, 61
Willie McGee Day, 2000, 73
Winter Warm-Up celebration,
    2002, 17, 19
The Wizard of Oz, 114
World Series, 1946, 135
World Series, 1968, 144, 156
World Series, 1972, 27
World Series, 1982
  Joaquin Andujar in, 5
  B. Forsch in, 9
  Game 1, 134–36, 138
  Game 2, 137–39
  Game 3, 5, 74, 138, 140–43,
      145, 157
  Game 4, 144–47
  Game 5, 148–52
  Game 6, xii, 13–14, 123,
      153–56
  Game 7, xii, 27, 31, 37, 68, 74,
      157–60
  Hernandez on, 37
  T. Herr on, 44–45
  Herzog on, xii
  D. Iorg in, 50
  Landrum in, 60
  LaPoint in, 64, 67–68
  McGee in, 74–76
  Oberkfell in, 84–86
  Darrell Porter in, 89
  Mike Ramsey on, 96
  Ozzie Smith on, 112
  Stuper in, 117, 123
  Bruce Sutter in, 130
World Series, 1983, 60
World Series, 1985, 7, 14
Worrell, Todd, 50

Y

Yale University, 117–25
Yatkeman, Butch, vi
Young, Dmitri, 94
Yount, Robin
  in 1982 World Series, Game 1,
      135, 136
  in 1982 World Series, Game 2,
      138–39
  in 1982 World Series, Game 3,
      142
  in 1982 World Series, Game 4,
      145
  in 1982 World Series, Game 5,
      148–51
  in 1982 World Series, Game 6,
      154
  in 1982 World Series, Game 7,
      159
youth sports, 87–89, 91